Many ecclesiological issues confront today's evangelical community; but glaring all of us in the face is an issue that perhaps is even more serious and foundational to the biblical message as well as the church's witness to the world—the character and qualifications of ministers of the gospel. The lack of serious self-criticism and sustained biblical analysis on this issue plagues the Christian house. This book by John Armstrong takes a sober look at this problem and endeavors to shake us into action to do something radical—that is engage the Bible obediently. The combination of biblical exegesis, theological reasoning, and historical discussion are all filtered through a pastor's heart that is wed to the glory of God and the power of the Gospel. Perhaps Dr. Armstrong's answer will provoke a renewed emphasis on the "goodness" of the ministerial office and the eternal significance of preaching the gospel.

Tom J. Nettles
Trinity Evangelical Divinity School

America is an increasingly pagan culture, and we can now see the curse of an increasingly pagan church. The scandals which have plagued American Christianity over the past decade have brought shame and disrepute upon the Church for which Christ died. When ministers of the gospel fall into sin, the integrity of the Church is called into public question. Armstrong has considered the issue in biblical, theological, and historical terms. He has left no stone unturned and yet he has thrown no stones at fallen brothers. The book reflects a properly pastoral tone and a broken heart. John Armstrong has sounded an alarm and we will ignore it to our peril.

R. Albert Mohler, Jr., President
The Southern Baptist Theological Seminary

CAN FALLEN PASTORS BE RESTORED?

THE CHURCH'S RESPONSE TO SEXUAL MISCONDUCT

JOHN H. ARMSTRONG

MOODY PRESS
CHICAGO

ISBN 0-8024-1412-5

1 3 5 7 9 10 8 6 4 2

Printed in the United States of America

To Anita,
my faithful wife of nearly twenty-five years,
whose excellence is beyond any human treasure I possess,
and whose heart I completely trust
(Proverbs 31:10–11). She has taught
me to take seriously what genuinely matters
and to laugh at what doesn't.

97/98

CONTENTS

*W*riting about fallen pastors and their possible restoration requires an author of compassion and understanding. John Armstrong demonstrates both qualities. He is no outsider: as a pastor he has served the church through good times and difficult times for more than twenty years. Though he writes with appropriate objectivity, he never is detached, because he well knows that the issues he discusses are of life and death importance to the church.

As a result, the book breathes deep compassion for the church and its spiritual leaders. The author's heart seems to ache with the words of Timothy Dwight's hymn "I Love thy Kingdom, Lord": "For her my tears shall fall; for her my prayers ascend."

The book is also courageous. An author invites misunderstanding and even risks vilification when he tries to cut through the therapeutic detritus common to today's thinking and question whether fallen pastors can be restored, and if so, under what circumstances. Because of his love for the church and ministry, Pastor Armstrong unflinchingly makes his case.

You will find this book to be conciliatory and irenic. There is no hint of the "Off with their heads!" spirit that can sometimes characterize theological disagreements. This is a pastoral letter from a sinner to sinners, composed with gracious humility.

Above all, *Can Fallen Pastors Be Restored?* is biblical. John Armstrong has done his homework, and the light of scriptural exegesis, church history, and careful reason illuminates the discussion. He rightly rejects the flawed reasoning that argues for restoration as a function of forgiveness. He also exposes the faulty reductionism of imagining that "adultery is like any other sin and the common thinking that restored pastors can become better pastors—"wounded healers" who are in touch with their people and more compassionate. Armstrong also raises the crucial character question, looking at the profound moral implications of hidden adultery by those in public ministry. At the same time, this work is truly therapeutic, as he offers the soothing balm of God's Word to bring wholeness to the church and her undershepherds.

The final virtue of the book is its wise counsel. Armstrong does not nail his theses to the modern church's door and walk away. He has solid, reasonable recommendations, informed by Scripture and experience, for the care of fallen shepherds.

Can Fallen Pastors is an important book on a crucial subject. In deserve a wide reading by pastors, denominational leaders, church elders, and all who love the church.

R. KENT HUGHES
Pastor and author of
Disciplines of a Godly Man

ACKNOWLEDGMENTS

Special thanks to the board of directors of Reformation & Revival Ministries, Inc., who serve me faithfully in the cause of teaching the church and serving its leadership. Our meetings always urge me to greater godliness.

This book could not have been written without the advice, counsel, and support of my pastor and dear friend, Kent Hughes, who shared the vision with me from the start and nurtured many ideas to completion.

Thanks, also, to John Sale, Don Whitney, Thomas J. Nettles, Thomas N. Smith and Erwin Lutzer, who read the first draft of this book and offered considerable input. None of these dear brothers will agree with everything I have said, but all of you have helped me say it better than I could have without you.

Every author needs an editor for a personal friend. For Donald Anderson, again I say "thanks" for all you do. You have encouraged me to write for almost twenty years now. You share in all I write and you give yourself cheerfully.

In the kind providence of God a friend urged James B. Newton to send me his doctor of ministry research project on "Pastoral Immorality" early in my research. Though Jim would not agree with everything I have said, I sincerely thank him for his help in this work.

Thanks to my family, who endure me working in their presence night and day—Anita, Matthew, and Stacy. And special thanks to Stacy, who is the best office assistant a father could have. You three are wonderful!

Finally, thanks to Moody Press for the desire to address an important topic like this one, especially to Jim Vincent, who has been a patient and superb editor, as well as Jim Bell and Linda Holland, who have been an encouragement to me as an author.

AFTER
THE FALL

*T*he call came in the night. I still remember the chills I felt as I hung up the phone. *How could this have happened? And to a much loved brother?* I asked myself as I drove to the meeting. Then I prayed, "Lord, this just can't be true! Assure me that he really has not fallen into sexual sin. I can't go through this again. I don't have the energy. My strength is gone."

Perhaps you can identify. Perhaps you have been there when a spiritual leader whom you put your confidence in fell into sexual sin. Maybe it was your pastor. Or maybe it was your best friend. Perhaps you went to college (or even seminary) together, or you had known each other since childhood. The awful news had come—your friend had been involved in sexual misconduct. The details held no interest. What remained so painful was the hurt you saw later in his eyes, the effect upon his whole body and soul. His very spirit ached so profoundly that you felt it. There is no way to relate to this, unless you've been there.

The headlines regarding sexual scandal in the church are all too familiar, but when you know the person, this is not headline news. This is personal tragedy, the kind that eats at a Christian's heart night and day. You really never get over it. You're never really the same.

If this happens to you, what do you do when you see him? All that you can do—you embrace him, weep with him, and listen with your heart. You don't ask, "How could you do this?" You don't probe into the nature of his moral collapse, and you certainly don't give your best sermon on the consequences of sexual sin and pastoral failure.

Perhaps as you visit with your friend the story comes to light slowly. This was a process, not a momentary slip. He was lonely, vulnerable, and weakened in his interior. He never expected such a fall to happen, especially to him. What he found out about himself is more than words can begin to express at this moment. He searches for phrases and an explanation, but little of either come from his lips. You realize time will allow for more personal reflection as the process of healing begins.

Has it happened to you? It has happened to me. I have wept and listened as my brothers cried. And I have been with pastors—Christian brothers—who have felt the Spirit's awful pressure upon their souls. (I also have been with some who have fought that pressure or felt it only slightly.) I remember one pastor who knew he was in deep trouble. He had experienced something that he would give the world to undo if only he could.

"Nathan hasn't fingered me, but the Holy Spirit is pressing me very hard," he told me. "My God, my family, our life, the church. I feel fear—a more than adequate salary and compensation will end; how can I provide? What has happened to me? How did I ever get into this wretched condition in the first place? I knew all the answers. I had helped many others. But I have fallen!"

This was not the time for moralizing lectures. Nor was it time for feeling good about myself because I hadn't fallen. This was a time for grief. Something precious and holy has been lost. All I could do was mourn the loss.

First and foremost, that is what we must do for such pastors—mourn the loss. Think about it. With sexual sin in the pastorate, lives are shattered. The pain will never fully depart. Before I even visited my friend, for instance, I realized that countless lives would be deeply affected when this sin becomes more widely known. *An esteemed pastor has become the ene-my's prey,* I thought. *His ministry is destroyed.*

It is time for Christians to unite to help our fallen pastors. But what should we do? We cannot lecture the fallen pastor, and this book contains no lectures. Instead this book responds as we must do as individuals: with compassion but also with a biblical love that holds Christian leaders responsible and restores them in a biblical fashion. What form such restoration takes is the subject of this book.

This requires a commitment on the part of each of us. I remember that as I listened to this pastor I began to realize that I would need to spend far more time with him than I had first imagined. I would need to meet him, and phone him regularly, and pray with him. This is accountability, which we will discuss in chapter 11. And there are issues the pastor must himself deal with, such as proper public confession, needed restitution, and realizing professional consequences.

But before any of this happens, we as a people must feel the pastor's hurt. Anger? Yes, but not at our Christian brother. What we should feel primarily is deep remorse.

If it's happened to you—hearing the shocking announcement of a leader's fall into sin—what did you do when you finally see him? You and I must come away from such an announcement or meeting overwhelmed with our own human weakness.

After I left this pastor, I pleaded with God to spare me, my family, and my church. I drove home tired, drained, and shaken to the depths. My body craved sleep but my mind would not turn off. Questions emerged so rapidly that I hardly had time to think clearly. "How will we tell his wife?" "How will we tell the church congregation?" "What about his long-term future?" Only much personal reflection, with considerable study and discussion, has yielded a Christian ethic of recovery.

And there is hope of eventual restoration. After many long years, one very dear friend who has been in the pit now glorifies God with a restored life and marriage. He describes the loss and calls on pastors to receive God's grace: "The question . . . is character and integrity. Yours are shattered. I plead with you, face the issue now! God's grace does restore. There is hope. However, that requires a process, much time, and even more grace. Confess, step down. Become accountable. Seek the cleansing and healing that you so desperately need. Do it this day. Do it now!"

The severe mercy of God must be appreciated for what it is, and for how it works in fallen and repenting pastors. As one fallen friend puts it: "My rampant sins of idolatry were exposed and needed to be dealt with. After all, it was my idolatrous thinking patterns on several fronts that fostered my sinful choices. I never knew they existed and it took my failure to reveal them to me. It will also take time to replace them."

Time. Yes, time. And loving support from trusted believers who will walk with you, the pastor, through the ordeal of restoration.

Yes, this book is written for pastors. But it also is written for lay leaders—elders, deacons, members of church executive committees—as well as every man and woman in the pew who are interested in the welfare of their minister and the advance of the gospel. We will look at the key Bible passages that deal with pastoral qualifications and possible disqualifications, performing exposition and exegesis of certain texts. But as noted above, our response embraces more than right action; it includes an attitude of humility and sorrow, and a desire to restore the pastor to usefulness to his family, his God, and even the church (perhaps in a different role, probably with a different congregation).

All of us who serve the church, either as pastors or lay leaders, must be willing to give of our time and our very lives for the recovery of fallen pastors and for the health of the body of Christ. May we invest ourselves as "servants for your sake" and thereby extend the mercy of Christ to all of those hurt by the tragedy of moral catastrophe in the pastoral ministry.

Nothing less than this spirit qualifies one to work for recovery in the area of sexual misconduct. May God grant this to many of His people, especially to me and you.

CHAPTER ONE

SCANDAL IN THE CHURCH

On the one hand, pastors are full-fledged members of the human race. They sin daily. On the other hand, pastors labor in a profession in which character is critical. They're called to lead and teach and model not some technical skill but a life. When pastors fall, they can wound many believers.

Marshall Shelley

*T*he story has become common—far too common. Another pastor admits to sexual sin. Fallen into adultery, he resigns in disgrace. Stories of adultery, especially with women in the congregation or even serving on the church staff, heads the list of the accounts of sexual failure by the clergy, but other sexually inappropriate behavior abounds: child molestation, pornographic activity, inappropriate touching, and homosexual acts, among others. Sexual sins have devastated more than pastoral ministries, too; leaders in youth groups, conference ministries, and high-profile parachurch agencies also have fallen. It seems as if we hear the account of another moral failure almost weekly.

But in the pastoral office the Christian church seems most seriously vexed by the problem of sexual misconduct. The scandals that attend the public announcements have repercussions that are deep and far-reaching. Over the past decade staggering revelations of the most sordid moral failure have rocked one congregation after another. No denomination, tradition, style of ministry, or geographical region has remained immune.

The media seem to continually splash before us stories of high-profile pastors who have fallen. Tabloid magazines and TV shows as well as serious periodicals report about recurring scandals in the church. Now, however, we are coming to realize that all of this is only the publicly exposed portion of an increasingly pervasive problem.

Time and *Newsweek* magazines recounted in the mid-eighties the lurid stories of widely known media ministers, and TV programs such as "Hard Copy" today seek and readily find accounts of ministers' moral failures. The monthly publication *Dallas* Magazine a few years ago devoted an entire issue to numerous charges against a young pastor in a large Baptist church in North Dallas. Leaders of the church had accused this minister of sexual liaisons with seven women in the church, including one divorced woman who claimed many affairs with this pastor over a four-year period. The minister was also accused of "lying, seduction, harassment, and greed." Subsequently the minister was arrested for stealing condoms, investigated by the Internal Revenue Service, and accused of embezzlement. Despite the charges by church and other local officials, he continued to preach in his church eight more months, finally resigning in complete disgrace.[1]

For all these widely reported scandals, scores of similar, lesser-known stories exist. During two brief years, for instance, one district in a conservative denomination I know had pastors resign from 10 percent of its churches because of sexual misconduct.

IS THE PROBLEM REALLY THAT BAD?

Is the problem of sexual scandal really that bad in the contemporary church? Haven't we always had this problem, but now it is "more out in the open" because of the impact of the news media?

Although no one seriously doubts that sexual sin has always been a problem among ministers, the extent of the present problem has made it a major, fast spreading, and almost incurable cancer in the body of Christ. What little research data presently exist bear out this observation.

In 1988 *Leadership,* a journal read mostly by ministers, conducted a poll on the sexual practices of clergymen and printed the staggering results in an article titled, "How Common Is Pastoral Indiscretion?" Based on more than three hundred responses from its readership, the survey revealed the existence of a growing moral breakdown in pastors' lives.[2]

Almost one in four pastors, 23 percent, answered yes to the question, "Since you've been in local church ministry, have you ever done anything with someone (not your spouse) that you feel was sexually inappropriate?" And 12 percent answered yes to this question: "Have you ever had sexual intercourse with someone other than your spouse since you've been in local-church ministry?" As a result, some have concluded that one in eight ministers is an adulterer. And of the 88 percent who said no to the same question, many confessed to having a great struggle in maintaining sexual purity.

If these statistics are not frightening enough, 18 percent of pastors responded that they had engaged in "other forms of sexual contact with someone other than your spouse, i.e., passionate kissing, fondling/mutual masturbation," while in local church ministry.

Similar research done by the Fuller Institute of Church Growth indicates that 37 percent of ministers "have been involved in inappropriate behavior with someone in the church." Harry W. Schaumburg, a therapist who works with problems of sexual misconduct and sexual addiction, adds to this statistic the following observation: "Evidence indicates that this shocking and disturbing statistic is true. I frequently receive calls for counseling from Christian leaders around the country who have 'fallen,' who are sexually addicted or have been involved in sexual misconduct."[3]

In the face of this painful problem many denominational leaders and high-profile pastors labor overtime for immediate damage control, and relatively early restoration to pastoral office, while others seek professional and psychological ways to address the problem before it ever occurs. Documents have been written by various church agencies addressing the issue of prevention. Others write on how to restore those who have already fallen. Some new counseling programs designed for fallen ministers are heralded as tools for positive change.

The *Leadership* survey of pastors found that more than two-thirds of the pastors had become sexually involved with people from within the congregation, often serving in leadership roles within the local church. Asked for the major reason for this illicit relationship, respondents most often replied, "physical and emotional attraction." After reviewing these results, one prominent counseling professor at a major seminary said, "We're living in a Corinthian age, but we're preparing students for the Victorian age."

Evangelicals might be inclined to think that adultery and other forms of sexual misconduct by clergy occurs only among the less theologically conservative fringe groups, or with the high-profile media preachers, but evidence suggests such conduct is far more pervasive. One religion editor, who devoted considerable study to this problem, recently wrote: "Experts who have studied clergy members' sexual misconduct believe at least one third of all ministers have committed some type of sexual abuse on members of their congregations—and the rate could be higher."[4]

SEXUAL MISCONDUCT HAS INVADED THE BIG-CITY SUPER CHURCHES, SMALL-TOWN PASTORATES, AND AT BOTH ENDS OF THE THEOLOGICAL SPECTRUM.

When clergy of several mainline Protestant denominations were polled ten years ago, 38 percent admitted sexual contact with members of their congregations. Researchers and counselors have expressed fear that the number may even be higher now.[5]

Baptist counselor Ray Woodruff, executive director of the 3,000-member American Association of Pastoral Counselors, modifies the figure slightly, yet admits the instances of sexual misconduct are increasing. "According to informed estimates, about fifteen percent (of clergy) either have or are violating sexual ethical boundaries," he says. "I don't think I would use the word 'epidemic' . . . but I suspect the number of incidents is increasing."[6] I would ask, if a virus were spreading through your community and affecting 15 percent of the population, would you consider it an epidemic?

While sex scandals among Roman Catholic priests have received the recent headlines, evangelical pastors and ministries are not immune. Counselors and denominational leaders now admit that sexual misconduct has invaded the big-city super churches, small-town pastorates, and at both ends of the theological spectrum.[7]

What have been the consequences of this sexual sin in the lives of those who participated in the *Leadership* survey in 1988? Only 6 percent said it resulted in divorce, with 16 percent saying it resulted in other marriage difficulties. Amazingly only 6 percent reported it cost them their job. Apparently this final 6 percent of respondents had reentered the pastoral ministry at some point after their sin, because the survey was confined to pastors presently in ministry. What staggers me is that 31 percent say their sin had no consequences, and only 4 percent said their churches found out about the sexual misconduct. I find the results even more disheartening than any of the previous data. Let me explain.

THE HIDDEN SIN

Almost one in five pastors (remember, this was still in 1988) confessed to sexual misconduct of some kind, with one in eight admitting adultery. Of this amazingly high number of unfaithful ministers only 4 in 100 were found out by their local church! Most of us hear stories of fallen pastors regularly. Yet these are only a very small fraction of what is actually going on. Thus hundreds of pastors who continue to lead churches battle incredible guilt and shame in their souls.

"What are these people doing with the guilt and the fear that they'll be found out?" asks professor and counselor Gary Collins. He believes that these men are being driven to one of two extremes. Their conduct "either makes them tentative, holding back even from healthy involvement with other people, or it leads them to preach strongly against sexual sin so the congregation won't suspect what they've done."[8]

Who can forget the harangues and condemnations of recently fallen media ministers who have railed against sexual immorality, with explicit language at times, only to find out that these very same men were guilty of lewd and perverse behavior. And, at the same time, who hasn't noticed the increasing absence of plain speech, of the kind that earnestly appeals to the conscience of the hearer, in our modern pulpits? We seem to have gone to one of two extremes. One wonders about the effect of private sin upon the minister, especially in the area of sexual purity. Without a clear conscience no man can meaningfully preach with discernible power to the conscience of others. Only with clean hands and a pure heart can the minister receive and give a blessing from the Lord. David, who knew what it was to fall sexually, wrote:

> Who may ascend into the hill of the Lord?
> And who may stand in His holy place?
> He who has clean hands and a pure heart,
> Who has not lifted up his soul to falsehood,
> And has not sworn deceitfully.
> He shall receive a blessing from the Lord
> And righteousness from the God of his salvation. (Psalm 24:3–5)

I am not suggesting that the absence of plain speech is solely the result of sexual misconduct in the life of the minister. I am suggesting that this might be a prominent reason, since the above research indicates that one in five ministers has fallen and only 4 percent have been found out by the church. How many men have run away from the scene of a failure, only to fall again? How many men have preached, with apparent effectiveness, for years, yet without God's power truly upon the message of the gospel?

And some Christian leaders seemingly are effective. The daughter of a well-known Christian minister years ago reported that her father had continually engaged in open verbal and emotional warfare with her mother (they were later divorced) right up until the time of services every Lord's Day. She related that when he entered the pulpit he was an entirely different person and was used with great blessing in the lives of hundreds of people, who believed he was a great man of God. This man remained in public ministry with seemingly significant approval ratings.

A FALLEN THOUGHT LIFE

Actual sexual misconduct is not the only issue in our pulpits. The *Leadership* survey found many pastors had fallen into the habit of fantasizing about sex with someone other than their wife. Six percent said they did so daily, 20 percent weekly and another 35 percent monthly or a few times a year. Of those, 39 percent did not consider such fantasizing harmful, even though Jesus clearly said such lustful thoughts are a form of committing adultery in the heart (Matthew 5:28). Noting their response, counselor Larry Crabb said, "I don't think those who consider sexual fantasies harmless really understand the deeper, compulsive nature of sexual sin."[9]

I recently heard a sermon by a fallen minister who openly longed to be restored to public ministry. When given the opportunity to speak, he proceeded to confess to fellow ministers that he never knew lust was itself a serious sin. I couldn't believe my ears! Here was a leading expository preacher, admired and listened to by thousands, who didn't seem to realize that lust was potentially a crippling, serious, and ministry-destroying sin. Then I pondered the previously cited research and was made aware once again that the Corinthian spirit of our present age has swept into the hearts of many of our pastors.

If such ministers are redeemed men, then their consciences surely must roar at them night and day. They cannot "do [their] best to maintain always a blameless conscience both before God and before men" (Acts 16:24), while at the same time entertain sin in their hearts and think of it as acceptable.

God alone knows how much damage these sexual sins have created within the contemporary church. We must sincerely fear when we realize that the reports in the secular newspapers and the Christian magazines form only a fraction of the overall problem. Harry Schaumburg has spent fourteen years helping what he calls clergy "sex addicts" and has had numerous counseling sessions with sexually fallen ministers. He observes:

> In recent years the church has been rudely reminded of a basic tenet: Christian leaders are not immune to sexual sin. The impact of the immoral behavior of people in key ministry positions can't be measured. I believe these well-known leaders who have fallen are but the tip of the iceberg, and that the problem of sexual addiction is widespread within the church. . . .
>
> These statistics don't reveal whether the pastors were sexually addicted or were just committing illicit sexual acts. But the evidence indicates that problems with sexual sin are rampant within the church, and more situations are sure to surface as more states enact laws against sexual exploitation and sexual violation of professional trust. The number of Christian people who call me for sexual addiction counseling is increasing, which is true of other Christian colleagues I talk with regularly.[10]

Many of my peers say, "It is bad, but not that bad!" The problem, they assure us optimistically, is that today we are more aware of such sin, whereas in the past it was there but not known to us. "This is a more open age, one where people are simply more public about their troubles and seek professional help. And that's good," they tell us. Sexually abusive pastors are not larger in number today, some argue, just more recognized, thanks to the diligence of the media.

I must ask you, as a church elder or deacon, or as a fellow pastor, "Do you really believe that this problem is not serious?" The levels of indiscretion are high and widespread. Furthermore, if you have studied church history, especially the eras of powerful reformation, the change should be apparent. Though not one account of a sexually fallen pastor is ever recorded in the New Testament, sexual sin was openly present in the church (1 Corinthian 6:18). Yet there is no mention of a pastor being overtaken in such a fault, and this in a first generation of new believers who were living in a sexually intoxicated society.

There can be little doubt that ours, too, is a sexually explicit culture, much like that in ancient Corinth. Though ministers have fallen in every age, perhaps even unnamed ones in the New Testament, where in collective memory can such public scandal be recalled by anyone living today? And remember, based on the available data that you have just read, we publicly know of only 4 percent of those who have fallen!

THE PERSONAL TRAGEDY

We cannot overestimate the untold hurt and agony brought about by sexual sin. Statistics do not tell the story. Ministerial sin, especially this sin, destroys both trust and respect. People have loved their pastor, listened to him with more than passing interest, and invested their lives with his. Some sins carry in them a heavy price; this is clearly one such sin. It violates the pastoral-congregational bond and destroys effective ministry. It sullies Christ's bride, the church, before a watching world, and it draws attention to everything but the gospel.

THE OVERWHELMING MAJORITY OF THESE FALLEN PASTORS . . . HAD HIGH SPIRITUAL GOALS [AND] ENTERED THEIR MINISTRIES LONGING TO SERVE AND TO HELP PEOPLE. THEY HAVE ENDED UP HURTING THE PEOPLE THEY WERE CALLED TO SERVE, AND THE DEEP PAIN THEY NOW FEEL IS THE RESULT OF FAILING BOTH GOD AND THEIR CHURCH.

The overwhelming majority of these fallen pastors began their ministries with a sense of divine vocation, or spiritual calling. They had high spiritual goals combined, usually, with much formal training. They entered their ministries longing to serve and to help people. They have ended up hurting the people they were called to serve, and the deep pain they now feel is the result of failing both God and their church. The reproach of their indiscretion will never go away, no matter how much help they get in coming days, or how much recovery they undergo through various therapies (Proverb 6:33).

It is not by accident that the apostle Paul refers to Timothy as the "man of God" (1 Timothy 6:11; 2 Timothy 3:17). In most churches mothers in the congregation have trusted their pastor to be faithful to them and to their children. They looked to this man to be a strong tower of moral purity. And single women have particularly honored this man as a role model for sexual fidelity. In a time when more and more women are struggling with the painful awareness of sexual abuse in their childhood they do not need a pastor they trust and love to become a sexual abuser.

Men, too, face grave difficulties when their pastor falls into sexual misconduct. They have led their families to public worship under the leadership of this man, trusting him in the administration of both the Word and the sacraments. They have prayerfully urged their families to hear God's still quiet voice through his preaching. They have respected him. No words can express the hurt, the loss, and even the anger that is often felt when scandal becomes public in the local church. Men, who desperately need the role model of a godly leader living above the sexual compromises of our age, will be severely tempted to lose hope that any man can remain pure. They are often, thereby, emboldened to sin because of what they see. And sexually tempted teenagers will often lose confidence that purity can really be preserved.

I recall the moral failure of an elder I knew very well. After he had sinned repeatedly and eventually given up all pretense to being a Christian, he shocked me by blaming a minister, claiming that the sexual infidelity of an area pastor had actually "opened the door in his mind" for his own moral indiscretion. Sin is brazen. It needs only a spark to light a huge fire. The indiscretions of ministers will be used to light many such fires.

EMPATHY AND JUDGMENT

The tragedies of scores of pastors, church leaders, and congregations transform our discussion from the theoretical to the personal. Whether you are an elder or deacon, a layperson or pastor, you probably recognize that this is an agonizing, personal problem. What can we do? It is important that we feel sincere empathy for the fallen. We will discuss the need for compassion throughout this book. It is also important to develop better counsel which will help restore broken and fallen shepherds.

But it is also time for us to acknowledge the divine principle "that judgment must begin with the household of God" (1 Peter 4:17). If we do not, we shall be collectively brought down to complete uselessness, as salt without saltiness, which is "thrown out and trampled under foot of men" (Matthew 5:13). Judgment is visited upon the entire family of God when a leader falls. Divine chastisement is administered to local churches in their corporate identity, even if few recognize this reality any longer. (Consider the seven churches in Asia Minor in Revelation 2–3.) The whole church must beseech God for mercies that will awaken us out of the moral sleepiness of a dark night. And we must respond to the present crisis with the Word of God as our only weapon, knowing that it alone is sufficient for all matters of faith and practice.

What is God's view of the fallen pastor? What does He have to say about this sin, about this pastor's future, and about his restoration? These are the questions I intend to address in this book. And there are other questions we will answer as well. How does God feel about what has happened to the local church, and to those abused by the adulterous pastor? What does holiness demand in the face of this moral crisis? Does forgiven mean ready to serve once again? Is forgiveness all that is necessary for a man to be a good minister of the gospel of grace? How important is moral purity, both past and present, for a man to hold the office of pastor/overseer? How should the church board respond to scandalous behavior, and why? How should denominations and independent local churches treat those ordained pastors who fall sexually after entering the ministry of the gospel? These, I believe, are often the ignored questions when we seek to address the problem of sexual misconduct in the church. Let's begin to answer those questions.

NOTES

1. Tim LaHaye, *If Ministers Fall, Can They Be Restored?* (Grand Rapids, Mich.: Zondervan, 1990), 13.

2. "How Common Is Pastoral Indiscretion?" *Leadership* 9 (Winter 1988): 12–13.

3. Harry W. Schaumburg, *False Intimacy* (Colorado Springs:NavPress, 1992), 180.

4. "Clergy Sex Abuse Is Widespread" *The Huntsville* (Alabama) *Times,* 14 May 1994, B–1.

5. Ibid.

6. "Pastors and Adultery," *The Illinois Baptist,* 5 January 1994, 6.

7. Ibid.

8. "How Common Is Pastoral Indiscretion?" *Leadership,* 13.

9. Ibid.

10. Schaumburg, *False Intimacy,* 149.

CHAPTER TWO

FORGIVE AND FORGET?

*Take no truth upon trust, but all upon trial. It was the glory of
[the Berean Church] that they would not trust Paul himself—
Paul, that had the advantage above all for external
qualifications—no, not Paul himself. Take no truth upon trust;
bring them to the balance of the sanctuary.*

Thomas Brooks

*A*s noted in chapter 1, any pastor can fall through sexual misconduct. What should your church leadership do when the pastor
has disgraced himself, his office, and his Lord? A God-ordained
trust was established through sacred vows and public ordination.
The call to serve this church brought with it high expectations
and godly hope. And when he became a husband, he vowed a life-
long commitment to sexual faithfulness during the wedding ceremony. During his ordination, fellow ministers placed hands on
him and the pastor pledged purity in the gospel ministry. Now
the pledge is broken, the trust is destroyed.

The contemporary church must navigate troubled waters,
and these are some of the most troubled. We must guard against
filling our little craft with the water of the world's ways. Tragically, today Western culture no longer largely views adultery as evil.
In the comprehensive 1994 study of sexual attitudes of American
men and women, *Sex in America,* University of Chicago researchers found 15 percent of women and 25 percent of men admitting
to having been unfaithful. More telling, almost one in four Amer-

icans (23 percent) disagreed with the statement "Extramarital sex is always wrong." They believe the violation of marriage vows is acceptable under certain conditions. (Amazingly, 80 percent of respondents condone sex before marriage; they disagreed with the statement "Premarital sex is always wrong.")[1]

A GROWING CONSENSUS

Those attitudes toward extramarital affairs seem to be infecting the church. As one said of our own time, "I looked for the church and found it in the world, and when I looked for the world I found it in the church." How shall those who guide the church respond to this present crisis?

The contemporary church has responded to this problem in a number of ways. It is relatively easy to outline these responses even though they vary in manner and application. In this chapter we will consider how many respond to the question of restoration of the fallen pastor. We will seek to determine if a consensus of approach actually exists.

AN OVERWHELMING CONSENSUS STILL EXISTS THAT MEN WHO FALL "SHOULD REPENT AND TURN TO GOD, PERFORMING DEEDS APPROPRIATE TO REPENTANCE" (ACTS 26:20B).

There is a consensus that fallen pastors need to repent. Not one notable pastor, author, or denominational leader I have consulted has suggested that a sexually fallen pastor should be kept in office if he does not repent of his sin. Furthermore, evangelical leaders seem to agree that whether the man has fallen only once, or numerous times over a period of many years, he must repent of his sin and renounce it. Most agree that he must renounce it in public as well as in private. Instinctively evangelicals are still aware of the truth of Peter's first-century counsel when he said, "Repent therefore and return, that your sins may be wiped away, in order that times of refreshing may come from the presence of the Lord" (Acts 3:19).

It seems an overwhelming consensus still exists that men who fall "should repent and turn to God, performing deeds appropriate to repentance" (Acts 26:20b). We seem to understand, even in an age where love has been almost singularly defined as benevolent goodwill toward all, that God says, "Those whom I love, I reprove and discipline; be zealous therefore, and repent" (Revelation 3:19).

After that, though, there is disagreement in answering one persistent question: "Should pastors guilty of sexual sin be reinstated to the office of overseer/pastor/elder?"

AREAS OF DISAGREEMENT

In the years I've studied the issue I have realized that evangelical leaders and churches seem to agree upon many things regarding an answer to this question. Yet for all of this agreement, several areas of disagreement remain, and they hinder a consistent practice regarding pastoral restoration.

Seriousness of the Sin

Many churches and leaders, for instance, disagree as to the seriousness of this sin, as well as the magnitude of the present problem. Churches, and sometimes their leadership, are often unaware of the patterns of such sin, the past problems the fallen pastor may have had in this area, and the present seriousness of his fall in terms of the people who have been abused.

Furthermore, church members and leaders are often ruled by the heart or the emotions. Ours is not an age known for deep thought. Often our society seems mindless, and the church tragically seems to follow this anti-intellectual direction. We often do not think through important issues and formulate consistent ethical responses.

Sexual misconduct in the pastorate gives rise to embarrassing complications and injuries that most church leaders and members feel incompetent to address. The general tendency seems to be "Don't rock the boat or it may make things much worse."

Limited Church Discipline

More and more churches are adopting policies regarding sexual behavior in leadership, both clergy and lay. Yet, at the same time, rare is the church that is willing to carry out church discipline, especially regarding a pastor, which is in accord with the teaching of Scripture (cf. Matthew 18:15–20 and 1 Timothy 6:19–20).

THREE COMMON APPROACHES

Assuming that the fallen pastor has expressed repentance and has broken off the sinful behavior that brought about his serious fall, restoration can be considered. Here are three common approaches to handle the problem of the fallen pastor:

1. Immediate restoration to pastoral office. "Immediate" is defined as fewer than twelve months after the sexual failure.

2. Future restoration to pastoral office after a period of time for counsel, as well as family and personal recovery. The procedure varies from church to church, but generally one to three years elapses before the fallen pastor is restored to pastoral ministry.

3. Personal restoration of the fallen pastor but with no possibility for restoration to office.

We shall consider the first two approaches in the remainder of this chapter. Whether one takes the first or the second approach, or some variation or modification of either of the two, the results will be the same. The forgiven pastor can be restored to office if he repents of his sin and seeks forgiveness.

Whether the process takes place immediately or over some prolonged period of time, it is then possible to restore him to his office. Under the first approach the pastor sometimes is never actually removed from the pastoral office, except very temporarily; at other times he may be suspended (whether formally or informally). If removed, he may then be reinstated to pastoral office, sometimes with a formal recommissioning service and a "laying on of hands" ceremony.

In many evangelical churches this restoration procedure does not involve a new process of ordination and/or reexamination of his life and doctrine as was done when he was ordained. He may take up pastoral service in the same church in which his moral collapse took place (or was first exposed to the public), or he may move to another location and begin anew there. Significantly, though, he is allowed, indeed we could say encouraged, to return to pastoral office and public ministry.[2]

APPROACH 1:
IMMEDIATE RESTORATION TO MINISTRY

Immediate restoration has been the approach taken in several highly publicized cases. The argument is that because God forgives all confessed sin—sin genuinely repented of—and because ministers are not inherently different from all other believers, immediate restoration is not only possible but desirable. Thus grace is believed to be openly displayed and the forgiveness of God's people received in the complete restoration of the fallen minister. In this scenario restoration always means restoration to office; this occurs fewer than twelve months after the sexual fall.

Several arguments are advanced to support this approach. We will study the six common ones.

Argument from the Life of King David

First, the repentance and restoration of King David is cited. As king of Israel who ruled over the people of God, David fell into serious sexual sin with Bathsheba, with whom he conceived a child. To that act he added the equally serious sin of murdering Bathsheba's husband, by putting Uriah in a place where he would be killed. Later, Nathan the prophet confronted the king and exposed his sin. King David's confession of wrong was both open and immediate, though it did not come until after the prophet had rebuked him.

One group of elders in a local church published a private document defending restoration to pastoral office which says:

> David's case is the classic Old Testament example (comparing with Peter's in the New Testament) of one who seriously failed in leadership but was reinstated. David's sins were lust, adultery and first degree murder. . . . It is crucial to realize how fully God restored David. It was after his restoration that God inspired David to write His Word (Psalm 51) and allowed David to father a son (Solomon) who would be in the messianic line (Matt. 1:6). Jesus is the "Son of David" . . . . not David, the innocent shepherd boy; or David, the hero; but David, the repentant adulterer and murderer!

Those church elders and many others argue that since David confessed his sin (Psalm 51:4) as being "Against Thee, Thee only . . . and [as having done] what is evil in Thy sight," his case parallels that of an openly repentant pastor under the New Covenant. David did not believe that God's forgiveness would be delayed by some "proving period" but rather it would be immediate and total. Nathan, after all, assured him in the counsel which he delivered, that because he had confessed his sin and repented of it, "The Lord also has taken away your sin; you shall not die" (2 Samuel 12:13).

David was restored to fellowship with God, and his throne was not taken away from him. He remained a leader over all of Israel. This is strong evidence, proponents argue, that God would have us keep a fallen minister in place if he immediately and openly repents and confesses his sexual sin.

Other Old Testament Examples

Second, other Old Testament cases can be cited of sins by godly leaders who were restored to ministry (though only one involved sexual misconduct). Moses and Aaron, for example, failed God but still led the people for a season. Samson repeatedly sinned against God sexually as he spent nights with women, including prostitutes. However, God still used him as a leader until he later broke the Nazirite vow by shaving his head (Judges 16:19–20).

Jacob, whose name meant "supplanter," was a deceiver, liar, and schemer who manifested almost complete self-will, yet he later was named by God "Israel" (meaning "prince with God"). Jacob became a patriarch, i.e., a father/leader in Israel. His grandfather, Abraham, lied regarding his wife and allowed her to be potentially violated sexually. He failed in a key area of integrity because of fear and a failure in his faith. Later, with his reputation ruined, he became "the father of the faithful" (Romans 4:16) and "the friend of God" (James 2:23).

In every case, it is argued, God forgave immediately when repentance occurred, and restoration took place there and then.

New Testament Examples

Third, proponents sometimes offer New Testament examples on behalf of immediate restoration to pastoral office. They cite the example of John Mark, rejected by the apostle Paul as unreliable but restored by Baranabas. (See Acts 13:13; 15:36–41; and 2 Timothy 4:11.) The primary example cited is the apostle Peter. As the document prepared by the local church referred to above puts it, "Peter would be the prime example of the grace of reinstatement. His sin of denying Christ with curses (oaths) would be the most serious of failures."

After Peter's threefold public denial the Lord Himself reinstates Peter to a position of leadership among the Twelve (John 21:15–23). It is argued that though Peter's sin was not sexual, it was indeed very serious, and in a very real sense it was of a similar nature in that he denied the Lord and brought disgrace upon both His servant and the office the Lord had assigned to him as an apostle.

It is not my purpose in this chapter to raise objections to these interpretations and illustrations but to merely state them as fairly as possible to show how this view is presented. We shall consider the different ways of understanding these texts and illustrations later.

God's Forgiveness and Ours

Fourth, because God forgives us of all sin, including sexual sins, the church should not withhold forgiveness from a man who repents and sincerely asks for forgiveness. The apostle John rightly says that "the blood of Jesus His Son cleanses us from all sin," and later adds, "If we confess our sins, He is faithful and righteous to forgive us our sins and to cleanse us from all unrighteousness" (1 John 1:7, 9).

The proponents again look at King David as a key example of God's total forgiveness of a sexually fallen and disgraced public leader. David wrote of his sin of adultery: "I acknowledged my sin to Thee, and my iniquity I did not hide; I said, 'I will confess my transgressions to the Lord'; and Thou didst forgive the guilt of my sin" (Psalm 32:5). And the same Psalmist rejoices that when he did confess his sin God promised to deal with it as follows: "As far as the east is from the west, so far has He removed our transgressions from us" (Psalm 103:12).

The apostle says that Christ was given for our salvation so that "He might redeem us from every lawless deed" (Titus 2:14). If this be true how can one argue that some lawless deed, such as sexual misconduct in a pastor, should be an exception?

Briefly, proponents of immediate restoration argue as follows: If God forgives all sin immediately, then we should forgive and restore to office the fallen pastor immediately. If not, we are refusing to do what God does, completely and totally forgive.

Equal Treatment of the Pastor

Fifth, keeping the pastor from further service is to treat him differently from any other member of the congregation. Yet the pastor is neither a priest nor the Chief Shepherd Himself. He is only a servant of Christ, to whom he will stand or fall. Proponents cite Romans 14:4: "Who are you to judge the servant of another? To his own master he stands or falls; and stand he will, for the Lord is able to make him stand." Often they will also refer to James 4:12: "There is only one Lawgiver and Judge, the One who is able to save and to destroy; but who are you who judge your neighbor?"

Their point is that the Scriptures made no distinction between the pastor and his congregation when it declared, "All have sinned and fall short of the glory of God" (Romans 3:23). Who can argue against the ministry of a pastor who has confessed his sin, repented of it according to the teaching of the Word of God, and desires to continue serving His Lord as a pastor? Surely if God called this man in the first place, He has not "uncalled" him now. If he truly confesses his sin and repents, we must allow him to continue his labors as a pastor or we are hindering the work of God in him and standing against the Holy Spirit.

The Nature of Sexual Sin

Finally, advocates of immediate restoration say sexual misconduct is not a worse sin than less obvious sins of the human flesh. The apostle Paul said the "deeds of the flesh are evident, which are: immorality, impurity, sensuality, idolatry, sorcery, enmities, strife, jealousy, outbursts of anger, disputes, dissensions, factions, envying, drunkenness, carousing, and things like these" (Galatians 5:19–21). Surely no one would argue that pastors escape the sins of jealousy and envy; thus, if immorality, impurity, and sensuality disqualify from pastoral ministry, then so do these sins. Sin is sin. We all sin and must continually confess our sin.

A Modern Case Study

A contemporary example of immediate restoration occurred in late 1993 when nationally known evangelical pastor David Hocking resigned his 6,000-member church in Southern California after what was termed a "moral failure." This removal, according to a report in *Christianity Today*, took Hocking out of the pastoral office as well as the membership of his church.

Less than four months after these revelations were made, Pastor Chuck Smith of Calvary Chapel, Costa Mesa, California, invited Hocking to join his church staff. One month earlier Smith and his church had placed David in "a supervised restoration process" that was to continue for one year.[3]

In extending the invitation to Hocking, Smith said, "This man is a gifted Bible teacher, and if he doesn't resume his teaching, I'm afraid he'll be literally and totally destroyed."

Hocking's former church addressed the discipline of David Hocking by saying, "We told Dr. Hocking that he couldn't serve in the ministry again. We told him he would never serve again, at this church. Dr. Hocking was to go through a restoration process, encompassing family and friends, but he has chosen to ignore our guidelines and follow his own."[4]

Pastor Chuck Smith later responded to a storm of criticism by writing a letter that was sent to hundreds of pastors in the Calvary Chapel movement. He referred to this letter as a "position paper." Smith began the letter by citing Galatians 6:1 as the basis for his actions. He explained,

> In light of this injunction, we are reaching out to David Hocking seeking to restore him and reinstate him to a place of service for our Lord. It goes without saying that God has gifted him in preaching the word. That he was taken in a sin, he has freely and openly confessed, and has repented of his sin. It is not necessary to know the details or the extensiveness of his transgressions, for they have already been forgiven by our gracious Lord.[5]

Pastor Smith then mentioned the actions taken in the discipline of David Hocking by his previous congregation, located just a few miles away, and describes their actions as "necessary according to the counsel they received from respected leaders in the Christian community." In explaining the addition of Hocking to the public ministry of Calvary Chapel within weeks of his discipline by his former church, Smith added:

> What is past is past, and what has been done has been done. Nothing is to be gained by continuing to bring up old issues that are covered by the blood of Jesus Christ. God has promised in Hebrews 8:12 that He would be merciful toward our unrighteousness, and remember our sin and iniquity no more. In Isaiah 43:25 God promised to blot out their transgressions for His sake, and would not remember their sins. If God remembers it no more, who are we to continually be bringing it up? The scripture tells us that love covers a multitude of sins, and again in Proverbs 17:9 it declares that he that covers a transgression seeks love, but he that repeateth a matter separates friends. To keep going back into the past and repeating David's sin will only create division in the body of Christ. Paul asks in Romans 8, "Who shall lay anything to the charge of God's elect? It is God that justifies, who is he that condemneth? It is Christ who has died, yea rather is risen again and is at the right hand of God who also makes intercession for us."
> The accusation has been leveled that David has not truly repented. Who knows David's heart to the extent that they can level such an accusation. Is this not the sin of judging which is condemned in the scrip-

tures? Have those who have leveled these accusations been with David in the all night sessions as David wept and agonized before the Lord for the reproach that he brought on the Name of Christ. Have they contacted David seeking in love to pray with Him and bear with him the heavy burden that he struggles under, realizing the shame that his sin has brought to the body of Christ? I know from the hours that I have spent with David that his tears continually flow. If David has not repented, then I do not know what repentance is.

The real issue is not the past, for that has been forgiven. But what about the future? The ministry of the Word of God has been David's life. He has been gifted by God in the teaching of the Word of God, and has blessed thousands through his exercise of this gift. Should this gift now be buried? Would God then hold him responsible for squandering the gift he has been given? Can David still bless those in the body of Christ by using his God given gifts? These are questions that only the Lord can truly answer, but I for one would not want to stand in the way of seeing David fully restored to the ministry.

The question I guess is how complete is the forgiveness of sins that the Lord offers to us. Jesus taught that if a man sins against us, if he repents, we are to forgive seventy times seven. Will the Lord's forgiveness be any less? The word justification means to be as though you had never done the evil. Is God's justification withheld from David? Is this a stain on David's life that cannot be removed by the blood of Jesus Christ? Jesus said to the Pharisees who brought the woman taken in the very act of adultery, "Let him that is among you who is without sin cast the first stone." That certainly disqualifies me from throwing stones. How full is the restoration that God offers, and how soon is God ready to restore? . . .

When Jesus restored Peter after his sin of denying His Lord, the question Jesus asked was, "Do you love me?" With Peter's positive response Jesus said, "Feed My sheep." Does David love Jesus? Of that I have no doubt. Then he should be feeding the sheep. And by the grace of God we are looking forward to his doing this in the future. We are planning to bring David on staff here at Calvary Chapel, his duties will include using his teaching gifts at our Bible School at Twin Peaks [A conference center and site owned by Calvary Chapel, Costa Mesa, Calif.]. He will also be teaching in our School of the Ministry.

As time goes on we will be giving him opportunity to teach in a week night class at the church and we will watch for the Lord to confirm His anointing upon His servant.

> Lovingly, a forgiven sinner, saved by grace,
> Pastor Chuck Smith[6]

Though it is not made clear in the above letter whether David Hocking was being *formally* restored to the actual office of pastor, this letter reflects most of the aforementioned aspects of the view that I have called "immediate restoration to office."

Whatever one thinks of this view it is apparent that Pastor Chuck Smith intends for David Hocking to be given a full opportunity for immediate public use of his pastoral gifts and ministry. One of the first activities David Hocking engaged in after this letter was mailed was the public teaching of the same pastors who received the letter. This was done at a gathering of Calvary Chapel pastors convened in Costa Mesa. At this meeting David Hocking spoke, with much sorrow, of his failure and of his experience of the pain of his sin and the grace of forgiveness.[7]

APPROACH 2:
DELAYED RESTORATION TO OFFICE
The Importance of Time

Most denominations, mission agencies, and local churches practice the second view: restoration to office after a period of counsel. They agree with the previous view in *theory,* but in practice they argue that time is needed for recovery to take place. This approach is more concerned with outward evidences of true repentance, with family reconciliation over time, usually involving professional counseling, and the complete disclosure of all necessary items related to the actual moral collapse itself. A concern for some type of restitution is usually built into the healing time, with concern for the redress of problems related to those sinned against by the pastor's indiscretion.

For our present purposes it is safe to say this approach argues that forgiveness constitutes the primary basis for restoration to office, though the reestablishing of outward character according to 1 Timothy 3:1–8 is made a factor of some importance.

This is the approach advocated by Tim LaHaye's helpful book, *If Ministers Fall, Can They Be Restored?* LaHaye, a respected pastor and counselor who offers none of the all too common excuses for sexual sin, believes most men who fail morally can be restored, with the time frame between the confession of the sin and the return to office varying widely due to the nature of the sin and what could be called the circle of offense.

LaHaye advances his thesis regarding the possibility of restoration to pastoral office by citing Galatians 6:1: "Brethren, even if a man is caught in any trespass, you who are spiritual, restore such a one in the spirit of gentleness; each one looking to yourself, lest you too be disqualified." LaHaye writes,

> . . . fallen ministers can under certain circumstances be restored to public ministry. The passage in Galatians specifically teaches restoration after sin. It doesn't specify what sin or what Christians, but it also doesn't exclude ministers taken in adultery. This text is aimed at restoring Christians who are living in sin at the time the restoration process is to begin taking place. Most of the conscientious ministers that I have dealt with are in a stronger position than that, having already ceased their immorality, repented voluntarily, and renewed their relationship to the Lord.
>   . . . . Since the Scripture gives no specific command prohibiting a fallen minister from returning to pastoral or pubic ministry, I would conclude that if over a period of time a minister faithfully meets the appropriate requirements for restoration, then he gradually should be allowed to assume whatever ministry the Holy Spirit opens to him —provided he submits to some form of accountability for the rest of his life.[8]

LaHaye argues, further, that "if only perfect vessels or those whose entire ministry was 'above reproach' were allowed to continue preaching, there wouldn't be enough qualified ministers to fill all the churches in one state—much less the fifty states and the rest of the world."

More Effective Ministry

This approach often stresses how truly effective the fallen minister can be if he confesses his sin. According to Kenneth Kantzer, distinguished professor at Trinity Evangelical Divinity School and former executive editor of *Christianity Today,* "Paradoxically, God sometimes permits us to fall into sin for our own growth and sanctification and ministry."[9] The idea is that a person like David was a better leader after he was damaged by his sin with Bathsheba because he had been broken by his failure. To use another popular idea, such men are now "wounded healers" or "broken shepherds" who out of weakness have been able to experience God's strength.

LaHaye also speaks of the "wounded healer" or "broken shepherd" as he describes the impact of a proper restoration: "A fallen minister can bring to his restored ministry a new brokenness and humility that God can use in other broken lives. In several cases, a fallen minister is an example to the believers (1 Corinthians 10:11) of the high price that must be paid for adultery." Then LaHaye adds a key qualification. "But even at best, *I do not believe his ministry will ever be the same*" (emphasis mine).[10]

Kantzer, like LaHaye, seeks to develop a compassionate and balanced understanding of this approach to restoration. He argues that some probably cannot be restored to office, but

> each decision represents a personal judgment for which we need the special illumination and guidance of the Holy Spirit. Often our decision becomes a delicate balance between a judgment as to the genuineness of the person's repentance and a quite different judgment as to what the fallen leader has learned from this experience that will enable him or her to do a *better* job and to be preserved from falling into a similar error. . . . The procedure for restoration must not be forced into a rigid pattern (emphasis mine).[11]

Qualifications for Restoration

Kantzer then offers a series of general guidelines that are much like those developed by LaHaye and other writers who advocate this view. Kantzer suggests that remorse, true confession, accountability, fruits that befit repentance, restitution, retreat, and a genuine call will all be part of the restoration to pastoral ministry process, if we are sensitive to the threads of doctrine that run through the Scriptures.

Kantzer concludes his thoughtful piece by writing:

> These guidelines, drawn generally from Holy Scripture, are not a rigid and invariable formula. . . . The sensitive Christian will seek to move toward reconciliation and restoration. But in doing so, he will take care not to devastate the moral and spiritual well-being of the one he seeks to restore. And he will be zealous for the health and safety of the church. The church will be stronger when we take more seriously what the Bible has to say about how we should treat those who have fallen.[12]

John Wimber, another highly visible pastor, opts for the same approach when he writes, "There is no question in my mind that fallen leaders can be restored. But saying restoration is possible raises a more difficult and complex question: what qualifications must they meet before they can be restored?"

Wimber takes a different approach than outlined by Chuck Smith. He reasons,

> When leaders fail we have a responsibility to love, forgive, and receive them back into the body of Christ, as we would any repentant sinner. But does genuinely forgiving their sin mean they should remain our leaders? If we fail to return leaders to office, does that mean we don't love them, that in fact we still hold their sin against them? In other words, does immediate restoration to ministry automatically accompany forgiveness? I think not. . . .
>
> [If the] sin itself were the only obstacle to leadership, restoration would be tied exclusively to receiving forgiveness. But far too often individual sins reflect the more troublesome problem of a flawed character. For this reason, repentance and forgiveness are prerequisites for entering the restoration process, not qualifications for completing the process. [13]

Most of the advocates of this second position would agree that fallen pastors need time and God's grace to work in their lives, powerfully building new patterns of righteousness and faithfulness, in order to reestablish their character.

Wimber, like Kantzer, suggests three useful questions to be applied to the fallen pastor during the process that might lead to his restoration to pastoral ministry: (1) Does the leader exhibit the fruits of true repentance? (2) Is the leader's sin the result of a momentary moral lapse or part of a habitual, cunning, and deceptive sin that reflects a seriously flawed character? (3) Is the leader accountable to others as he works through the restoration process?[14]

LaHaye adds several observations about the "cost of restoration." They are: (1) Restoration should be determined by the fall. (2) The way of the transgressor should be hard (Proverbs 13:15). (3) Restoration is risky business. He concludes by admitting that among the men he has watched after restoration, "None of them, however, is experiencing the ministry he would have enjoyed if he had never committed sexual sin."[15]

THE CONSENSUS:
RESTORE TO PASTORAL MINISTRY

A consensus of evangelical opinion seems to have developed around the answer to the question, "Can fallen pastors be restored?" Most agree that they can be restored, not only to the church visible, but also to the public ministry of Word and sacrament and thus to the office of pastor. This consensus seems to have developed over the past several decades based upon the common idea that repentance and forgiveness open the door for the sexually fallen pastor to return to ministry. The period of time argued for varies, from almost immediately to a period of one to three years; others do not wish to be specific but feel time is important for re-qualifying the man's character before the church and the world.

Four pastoral leaders expressed their views on restoration in a roundtable discussion reported in the journal article entitled "How Pure Must a Pastor Be?" (*Leadership*, Spring 1988); most agreed with this consensus view.

Donald Njaa, executive director of the ministry, the Evangelical Covenant Church of America, expressed well the consensus view when he spoke of his own denomination's approach by saying, "Our rules say we're to be restorative if possible. Ministers who get themselves in trouble know they can eventually be cleared and free to reenter ministry. There are many examples of that." Later, when Charles Swindoll argued that a pastor's character is seriously flawed through sexual failure and that this could disqualify him from future pastoral service, Njaa replied, "I'm not sure I agree with the notion of a character flaw. Sin is sin; I don't think there is anything deeper. Christ died to atone for sin. As a result, it's very possible for someone who has sinned deeply to be restored—even to ministry."[16]

Expressing a similar idea in the same discussion was Eugene Peterson, now professor at Regent College, Vancouver, British Columbia:

> I guess my basic feeling is that there's nothing that *disqualifies* [italics added] us from ministry. Everything is redeemable. Scripture brims with

that. Moses was a murderer and he kept on. Abraham forced his wife into adulterous relationships—or at least was willing for that to happen. . . . I do think we have to be careful, though, when we use the word *disqualification* for ministry. I don't think there is any (emphasis mine).[17]

The comments of Peterson and Njaa reveal quite clearly what has become the consensus approach toward pastoral restoration in our day. Forgive and forget, either immediately or sometime in the not too distant future, has been established as the evangelical approach in most churches and ministries.

Books have been written, seminars offered, and moving testimonies of full recovery and complete restoration to pastoral ministry given. Many of God's people, however, have nagging doubts about offering every repentant pastor full restoration to pastoral ministry. Arguments that fallen shepherds are "wounded healers" and thus better able to minister out of their experiential human weakness trouble those who believe that the Chief Shepherd never needed to fall morally in order to fully sympathize with our humanity and weakness (Hebrew 4:15). Indeed, the fact that He was tempted as a Shepherd and did not fall is the actual source of much encouragement to believers, who can, with His divine help, resist temptation and remain morally strong and sexually pure. If the model and example for the undershepherd be compromised so easily, one must ask what will become of the human "living letters" that Paul said we should all be known as, and that all outsiders can read (2 Corinthians 3:2). Thus the third approach has its proponents, and I will argue for its superiority to the first two views in future chapters.

Whatever your view, I hope that you will stay with me as I seriously question the reasons given for this consensus. What we do with this issue may well determine our corporate commitment to the recovery of our lost purity in the church. I believe that the Lord is saying to thousands of congregations in the West: "I advise you to buy from Me gold refined by the fire, that you may become rich, and white garments, that you may clothe yourself, and that the shame of your nakedness may not be revealed; and eyesalve to anoint your eyes, that you may see" (Revelation 3:18). We are, in the sight of the sovereign Christ, much like the church in ancient Laodicea, "wretched and miserable and poor and blind and naked. . . "(3:17). Our future spiritual prosperity may well be related to how we answer this question of pastoral purity and integrity.

NOTES

1. Philip Elmer-Dewitt, "Now for the Truth About Americans and Sex," *Time* , 17 October 1994, 64; and Peter Gorner, "What Is Normal?" *Chicago Tribune*, 9 October 1994, 4:1. *Sex in America*, published by Little, Brown, is the popular version of the comprehensive survey and analysis *The Social Organization of Sexuality* (Chicago: Univ. of Chicago, 1994), by Robert Michael, John Gagnon, Edward Laumann, and Stuart Michaels. June 1989.

2. Many of the historic mainline denominations, though generally more theologically liberal, have seemingly done a better job in openly addressing the problem of pastoral sexual misconduct itself, in writing policy and procedural documents on how to respond to the issue, and in general taking seriously that there really is a major problem in the contemporary church.

3. Personal correspondence from Chuck Smith, 29 September 1994.

4. "Ousted Radio Pastor to Join Calvary Chapel Staff," *Christianity Today,* 8 February 1993, 54.

5. A general pastoral letter mailed to the pastors of congregations associated with the Calvary Chapel movement, January, 1993.

6. Ibid.

7. A cassette tape of an address given by Dr. David Hocking to the pastors of Calvary Chapel congregations given in Costa Mesa, California, March 1993. In this tape Hocking expresses sorrow over his moral failure and gratitude that Chuck Smith has given him a new opportunity for public service through the use of his preaching/teaching ministry.

8. Tim LaHaye, *If Ministers Fall, Can They Be Restored?* (Grand Rapids, Michigan: Zondervan, 1990), 160–161.

9. Kenneth Kantzer, "The Road to Restoration," *Christianity Today,* 20 November 1987, 20.

10. LaHaye, *If Ministers Fall,* 161.

11. Kantzer "The Road to Restoration," 21.

12. Ibid.

13. John Wimber as quoted in *Equipping the Saints,* Summer 1988, 3.

14. Ibid., 4, 6, 22.

15. LaHaye, 167.

16. "How Pure Must a Pastor Be?" *Leadership,* 9 (Spring 1988): 12 ff. The roundtable discussion featured four Christian leaders seeking to answer the question. Those men were Eugene Peterson, Charles Swindoll, G. Raymond Carlson, and Donald Njaa. Only Swindoll differs significantly from the consensus view that men are not disqualified in some way by virtue of their sexual misconduct.

17. Ibid., 17.

CHAPTER THREE

ALL SINS ARE NOT CREATED EQUAL

The sins of the godly are worse than others, because they bring a greater reproach upon religion. For the wicked to sin, there is no other expected from them; swine will wallow in the mire; but when sheep do so, when the godly sin, that redounds to the dishonor of the Gospel: "By this deed thou hast given great occasion to the enemies of the Lord to blaspheme."

Thomas Watson

*A*t the end of *Animal Farm,* George Orwell's classic satire, the Seven Commandments for life have been reduced to one. That final rule reads: "All animals are equal, but some animals are more equal than others." Unlike the situation on Animal Farm, most Christian Protestants would agree that when it comes to sins committed against God, all sins are created equal. We reject the Roman Catholic doctrine of venial (lesser) sin and mortal (damning) sin. All sin is sin that makes us unworthy of God, and our only deliverance—which is complete for every sin—comes through the atoning sacrifice of Jesus.

As a result, many believe that sexual immorality in general, and adultery in particular, are no different than other sins. Some, wishing to apply the teaching of Jesus in the Sermon on the Mount, even argue that there is no essential difference between mental adultery, what Jesus calls "adultery in [the] heart" (Matthew 5:28), and the actual physical act of adultery, since both bring the same condemnation referred to in the text. And both are plainly called adultery by Jesus Himself.

Their logic proceeds this way: If all have committed mental adultery, then who is able to judge his fellow Christian or pastor for actually committing physical adultery? This kind of thinking is implicit in the comment of one notable, fallen pastor who said, regarding the discipline administered by the church in which he failed, that "I feel like sending a basket of rocks over to them." What this pastor said candidly to an interviewer about those without sin casting stones (cf. John 8:7) many have said less candidly, or at least implied.[1]

Christianity Today editor David Neff responds to such thinking in his article "Are All Sins Created Equal?" where he writes:

> Whenever a Christian leader is discovered to have carried on a clandestine affair, a self-assured voice emerges among the gasps and sniggers. "Let us remember, it says that all sin is equally heinous before God. Sexual sin is no different. We are all sinners, and in God's eyes we are as guilty as our fallen brother or sister."[2]

This seems reasonable, of course. Such thinking, though, causes church congregations to accept a leader with a mean streak, or learn to live with a visionary who subordinates accounting procedures to his pet projects. Such thinking not only begs vital moral questions, but it fails to come to grips with some significant matters, biblically and ethically.

Are all sins really the same? Should we respond with the simplistic, but all too common nostrum, "Sin is sin, what real difference does it make?" David Neff's short article and my own subsequent biblical and theological study have convinced me that the answer, very plainly, is no!

In this chapter we will see why sexual immorality has such serious and lasting consequences that its reproach never fully departs in this life (Proverbs 6:32–33). The damage a minister creates is not only against the Lord, but against people: his wife, his children, and the other woman's husband, if she is married. The sin is also against the local church, the visible bride of Christ on display before the world, and directly against the Lord of the church who holds those who teach to a greater requirement in every way (James 3:1). The apostle James says that those who teach "shall incur stricter judgment (or great condemnation)."

ADULTERY: A GREAT SIN

Most of us recognize that certain sins carry in them a type of inherent judgment. If a person is lazy, for example, he will generally not prepare for the future and will ultimately suffer the consequences of his own laziness.

Sexual infidelity, like other sins that violate people made in the image of God, brings with it not only long-term consequences but direct judgment from God Himself. The evidence begins with the Scriptures, the underpinning of the Christian church. The writer to the Hebrews warns of God's judgment as he describes the marriage relationship: "Let marriage be held in honor among all, and let the marriage bed be undefiled; for fornicators and adulterers God will judge" (13:4). Adultery is one of those sins that defrauds and brutally violates others directly. Adultery is not simply a "slip-up" but a massive, often planned, rebellion. This is part of what is behind Paul's counsel when he writes:

> For this is the will of God, your sanctification; that is, that you abstain from sexual immorality; that each of you know how to possess [or acquire] his own vessel [or wife] in sanctification and honor, not in lustful passion, like the Gentiles who do not know God; and that no man transgress and defraud his brother in the matter because the Lord is the avenger in all these things (1 Thessalonians 4:3–6).

When Paul refers to a brother being defrauded in this matter, he is surely referring to the kind of lust and avarice that destroys another believer. He also may be referring to what happens when a brother sexually violates another through the sin of adultery with another man's wife. This interpretation was actually held by some of the early church fathers, though it is not favored by all today. Either way we understand Paul's reference to "defrauding;" God personally is involved in becoming "the avenger" when one brother violates another. If this is true of the kind of avarice that works havoc in another's life economically then it surely would include a more direct violation of the brother's humanity through sexual sin.

What is staggering is this: Paul says that when another is sinned against in a way that defrauds his person, God acts directly as the avenger against the sinning party.

> *WHEN WE COMMIT SEXUAL SINS WE SIN MOST DIRECTLY AGAINST GOD'S ORDERED PLAN FOR CREATION, AND HIS AWESOME HOLINESS. WE AGGRESSIVELY ATTACK HIS HOLY NAME . . . AND HIS HOLY LAW.*

In addition, to understand the nature of sexual sin in marriage, we must note how Paul uses the word "sexual immorality" in verse 3 (as he does in other Scriptures). "Sexual immorality" is the translation of one word, *porneia*. Unlike *moicheia*, the Greek word for adultery, *porneia* is a more general word for any kind of sexual misconduct. Originally the word described prostitution by female slaves, but in later Greek it meant sexual deviation of any kind, including adultery. As a result, most scholars agree that Jesus' so-called exception clause permitting divorce (that is, the acceptable grounds of ending a marriage by the party who has been sinned against) in Matthew 5:32 and 19:9 is *unfaithfulness to the marriage vow through any kind of sexual expression that breaks the marriage bond*. Such unfaithfulness violates the covenant made by the two parties in marriage.

This indicates that sexual sin in marriage that constitutes adultery is much more than physical intercourse with a woman other than one's wife. Sexual unfaithfulness to the marriage covenant includes several sexual sins—all that attack the covenantal oneness inherent in fidelity to one's marriage partner. These include deviate sexual behavior which is increasingly rampant in our time. Thus when I refer to sexual misconduct in my arguments I am using the term the same way that Protestant exegetes have used it, following the tradition of Calvin, Luther, and the Reformation tradition.

God gave marriage to mankind as a good gift. When this gift is abused in sexual immorality, man rejects God's goodness, wisdom, and generosity. The immensity of this offense arises from several important considerations.

First, marriage is sacred. It is a covenantal relationship. God gave it to mankind directly, as an ordinance of creation. We have been given many good, common, and ordinary gifts; most are part of the created order of things. But none of those gifts can be thought of as creation ordinances like marriage, in which God's intention is to display His most abundant blessing to mankind. By using the term *sacred* I mean "dedicated to or set apart for" the worship and service of God.

Thus when we commit sexual sins we transgress directly against God's ordered plan for creation and His awesome holiness. We aggressively attack His holy name, His holy character, and His holy law. "The adulterer," wrote Puritan theologian Thomas Watson, "sets his will above God's law, tramples upon his command, affronts him to his face; as if a subject should tear his prince's proclamation. The adulterer is highly injurious to all the Persons in the Trinity."[3]

Second, adultery is a huge sin because of the holiness of the commandments of God and the great dishonor it brings against the author of those commandments. The seventh commandment is most explicit, and following the sixth it implies that just as murder destroys or takes another person's life, so does adultery.

Thomas Watson wrote,

This commandment is set as a hedge to keep out uncleanness; and they that break this hedge a serpent shall bite them. Job calls adultery a "heinous crime" (Job 31:11). Every failing is not a crime; and every crime is not a heinous crime; but adultery is a *flagitium*, "a heinous crime."[4]

With Watson, I argue that adultery "is committed with mature deliberation," and is not simply a shortcoming or "simple fall" of the moment, as many are prone to say. Watson elaborates on this point by adding, "[In adultery] there is contriving the sin in the mind, then consent in the will, and then the sin is put forth into act."[5]

Third, adultery not only wrongs the soul of one person but also violates another. It jeopardizes the soul of another human, who is engaged in the act, and it threatens the souls of others affected by the act directly or indirectly. Watson says:

LUST, JEALOUSY, PRIDE, AND HATRED ARE DAMNING SINS, AND IF UNREPENTED OF WILL JUSTLY SEND A PERSON TO HELL. . . . [BUT] THEIR OUTWARD PHYSICAL MANIFESTATIONS . . . ADULTERY, FORNICATION, AND MURDER—ARE MUCH GREATER SINS.

[Adultery] kills two at once. He is worse than the thief; for, suppose a thief robs a man, yea takes away his life, the man's soul may be happy; he may go to heaven as well as if he had died in his bed. But he who commits adultery, endangers the soul of another, and deprives her of salvation so far as in him lies. Now, what a fearful thing is it to be an instrument to draw another to hell![6]

Fourth, adultery destroys trust like few other sins. "Dalliance destroys trust," writes Neff. "Before the adultery comes the marriage. . . . Short of baptismal promises, the marriage vows are the most comprehensive vows a Christian can make. When the dike is breached by adultery, spouse and children can drown in the tide of pain. And the ripples and eddies of hurt reach far beyond the immediate family." Indeed, the heart of true leadership is trust, reliability, truthfulness. When adultery takes place the adulterer "violates trust in a fundamental and public manner [and] is ipso facto no longer a leader."[7]

Fifth, like few other sins, adultery destroys personal reputation (Proverbs 6:32–33). It is a frightful thing to contemplate a reproach that will never be wiped away in this life. Watson warns, in a manner rarely heard in modern discussion: "Wounds of reputation no physician can heal. When the adulterer dies, his shame lives. When his body rots underground, his name rots above ground." [8]

In summary, I wish to argue for a position that agrees with the general, historical interpretation of the church and traditional moral theology. The position is this: Although lust, jealousy, pride, and hatred are damning sins, and if unrepented of will justly send a person to hell, their outward physical manifestations—adultery, fornication, and murder—are much greater sins. Why? Because they (1) greatly damage the name of God and (2) the character and lives of the persons involved, and (3) bring woeful effects upon the church to which the adulterer belongs.

Therefore, acts of sexual immorality are more severe in consequence than the heart sins that precede them. The heart sins, unless repented of, may very well lead the person to act upon his inner desires. Heart sins are detestable to God. But God's Law is quite specific about His holy hatred for sexual impurity in deed, especially by those who openly profess love to His name. The penalty for violating the seventh commandment and several sexual sins was death in Old Testament times (Leviticus 20:10–16), and Jesus and New Testament writers repeat the injunction against adultery in the New Testament (Luke 18:20; Hebrews 13:4).

Further, adultery is a greater sin because it attacks the very essence of marriage and allows the party who has been sinned against to pursue divorce, if he or she so chooses (Matthew 19:9). The mental counterpart, i.e., "heart adultery," will provide the soil in which the acts of adultery will grow, but mental adultery does not directly end a marriage. Adultery physically violates another's body (and we shall shortly consider this more particularly); but mental adultery does not. Adultery may eventuate in illegitimate births; mental adultery does not.

MENTAL ADULTERY VS. PHYSICAL ADULTERY

There are major, substantive differences between mental adultery and the physical act of adultery. The differences parallel those of hatred or other misplaced passions (anger and bitterness, for example) and the actual act of murder. Mental murder (Matthew 5:22–23) occurs regularly, and with baleful effects upon many. But when hatred leads a person to murder, a life is taken, a family is grieved, and the social fabric of society is permanently ripped a bit further. Chaste believers must never allow the adulterer's—or the murderer's—cliché defense, "Your sin is just as great as mine," to cloud their thinking or their actions.

ALL SIN WILL LEAD A MAN TO DESTRUCTION, UNLESS REPENTED OF AND FORGIVEN, BUT NOT ALL SIN IS EQUALLY WICKED, EITHER BEFORE GOD OR MAN.

Those who misinterpret James 2:10 to minimize the heinousness of adultery, rationalize that there are no gradations of sins, and that one sin is as bad as another. But when the apostle writes "For whoever keeps the whole law and yet stumbles in one point he has become guilty of all," he is saying, simply, that the whole of God's law is a seamless garment. It takes only one rip to tear the whole of the garment. One broken law rends the whole law. This means, quite simply, that when one lies, for instance, he is not guilty of adultery, but he has broken the whole of God's law in the sense that he is a lawbreaker in thought, word, and deed. He is condemned before the law and only by the gospel can he find hope and forgiveness.

What Bible scholars call "contemporary reductionism" threatens to confuse us in this matter. Instead, we must recognize that all sins are acts of treason. Having said this, we also must recognize that certain sins are "high treason" in a very real sense. All sin will lead a man to destruction, unless repented of and forgiven, but not all sin is equally wicked, either before God or man. And when the sin is committed by one who aligns himself with Christ as His disciple the magnitude is not less, but greater, as we will now see.

THE SIN AGAINST ONE'S BODY

The immensity of adultery and its cataclysmic effects seemingly cannot be overstated in the light of the powerful theological expression of the apostle in 1 Corinthians 6. Here Paul argues that adultery is an even greater sin than many other sins because of its direct effect upon the body of those involved in the sin. Ponder his inspired word:

> Flee immorality. Every other sin that a man commits is outside the body, but the immoral man sins against his own body. Or do you not know that your body is a temple of the Holy Spirit who is in you, whom you have from God, and that you are not your own? For you have been bought with a price: therefore glorify God in your body (18–20).

Sexual relationships affect the union between a man and a woman wherein they become "one flesh" (Genesis 2:24). As a covenantal relationship, marriage is the act of becoming one flesh, according to Adam, who called Eve "bone of my bones, and flesh of my flesh" (Genesis 2:23). Bruggemann sees Adam's words as describing this covenant relationship, writes commentator Victor Hamilton:

> Bruggemann argues that the phrase "my/your bone and flesh" is actually a covenant formula and that it speaks not of a common birth but of a common, reciprocal loyalty. Thus when representatives of the northern tribes visit David at Hebron and say to him, "we are your bone and flesh" (2 Sam. 5:1), this is not a statement of relationship ("we have the same roots") but a pledge of loyalty ("we will support you in all kinds of circumstances"). Taken this way, the man's *this one, this time, is bone of my bones and flesh of my flesh* becomes a covenantal statement of his commitment to her. Thus it would serve as the biblical counterpart to the modern marriage ceremony "in weakness [i.e. flesh] and in strength [i.e. bone]." Circumstances will not alter the loyalty and commitment of the one to the other.[9]

Thus the act of adultery breaks this God-given covenant and the pledge of loyalty that is inherent in it. An oath made to God and another person is violated. It involves the one who so sins in a number of other serious sins that always attend its sad choice. Commentators are agreed that the essential meaning of this "one flesh" idea referred to above is sexual union. This physical union is a consummation of the covenant between the man and his wife. Theologian Sinclair Ferguson recognizes this fact when he writes: "The powerful sexual drives which are built into man's relationship with woman are not seen in Scripture as the foundation of marriage, but the consummation and physical expression of it."[10] When a person chooses sexual immorality over covenantal loyalty he chooses to attack and undermine both the God of the covenant and the person he pledged to love and protect. He sins further against his own body, and that in a most profound way, as we will see.

When Paul wrote that "the immoral man sins against his own body," the apostle made a distinction between sexual immorality and other sins. Most exegetes, beginning with John Calvin, see this distinction clearly. The Protestant reformer defended this comparative view, when he wrote:

> Having set before us honourable conduct, [Paul] now shows how much we ought to abhor fornication, setting before us the enormity of its wickedness and baseness. Now he shows its greatness by comparison—that this sin alone, of all sins, puts a brand of disgrace upon the body. The body, it is true, is defiled also by theft, and murder, and drunkenness. . . . Hence some, in order to avoid this inconsistency, understand the words rendered against his own body, as meaning against us, as being connected with Christ; but this appears to me to be more ingenious than solid. Besides, they do not escape even in this way, because the same thing, too, might be affirmed of idolatry, equally with fornication. For he who prostrates himself before an idol, sins against connection with Christ. Hence I explain it in this way, that he does not altogether deny that there are other vices, in like manner, by which our body is dishonoured and disgraced, but that his meaning is simply this—that defilement does not attach itself to our body from other sins in the same way as it does from fornication. My hand, it is true, is defiled by theft or murder, my tongue by evil speaking, or perjury, and the whole body by drunkenness; but fornication leaves a stain impressed upon the body, such as is not impressed upon it from other sins. According to this comparison, or, in other words, in the

sense of less and more, other sins are said to be *without the body*—
not, however, as though they do not at all affect the body, viewing
each one by itself. "

Modern scholars are in general agreement with Calvin.
C.K. Barrett, for example, admits that these words "raise a difficult exegetical problem." He observes:

> A distinction is made between fornication and all other sins in respect
> of their relation to the body. Is this distinction valid? . . . Fornication
> is a sin not only against God, and not only against the other person
> involved, but against the fornicator's own body, which is designed to
> belong not to a harlot, but to the Lord (verse 13), and is wronged if
> devoted to any other end.[12]

Bible commentators and early churchmen alike agree
adultery can enslave and will appeal to the individual's imagination and personality. "Other vices are overcome by resistance," wrote Thomas Charles Edwards, a nineteenth-century
British scholar. "The imagination detracts from the fascination
of other sins, but adds fuel to the flame of fleshly lusts. . . .
[The church father] Ambrose wrote, 'I have fled from lust, as if
I were fleeing from a savage and fierce master.'" Edwards offered the most likely meaning for Paul's concern that sexual
immorality is "against the body" by saying, "The meaning is
that fornication institutes a relation which affects the sinner's
personality" (emphasis added). [13]

Here is the point that gets to the heart of Paul's concern.
Sexual sin is a sacrilege. It defiles and flagrantly assaults the
temple of God, for as the apostle writes, "Your body is a temple
of the Holy Spirit who is in you" (6:19). Edwards is again helpful when he writes:

> The Apostle alludes indirectly to the contrast between the dwelling-
> place of a holy God and the temples of heathen deities, in some of
> which fornication is itself a sacred rite. . . . The difference is
> noteworthy between the Apostle's declaration that the body is the
> shrine of the Holy Spirit and the philosopher's description of it as a
> prison and a tomb.[14]

Paul presented what are undeniable facts as he compared sinful acts in general with sexual sin in particular. Beginning at 1 Corinthians 5:1 he had addressed the problem of sexual misconduct in the Corinthian church; next he prepared the ground for what now comes in this particular text. R.C.H. Lenski, a prominent Lutheran scholar best known for his massive commentary series on the New Testament, argues that Paul here

> really states the major premise of a syllogism: Fornication, *as does no other sin,* violates the body. The minor premise will follow: The Christian's body is the Spirit's sanctuary. And then the conclusion of this syllogism is plain: Fornication, *as does no other sin,* desecrates the very sanctuary of God (emphasis mine).[15]

Sexual sins bear a character all their own. Writes Lenski,

> They are peculiarly unsavory and hence entail shame and disgrace in a peculiar manner. They rot the body, fill the mind with rottenness, and rapidly eliminate the sinner from this life. . . . We err also when we question or challenge Paul's statement regarding the exceptional character of fornication by referring the exceptional character to a sin like suicide or others that damage the body like drunkenness, gluttony, addiction to drugs, etc. Paul is far more profound: *no sinful act desecrates the body like fornication* and sexual abuse. In this sense fornication has a deadly eminence (emphasis mine).[16]

By virtue of the Holy Spirit's indwelling, the body of the true believer has become a temple. The apostle argues that the sanctuary within is desecrated by sexual sin, and thus the whole temple is radically affected by this foul rebellion. All other sins attack from without the sanctuary, in the way that they affect uman person and his personality. In contrast, sexual sin attacks the inner sanctuary in a profound way, hurting the personality and defiling the outer temple, his body.

Does this mean that sexual sin cannot be forgiven? Is this, then, the *unpardonable* sin? In the same chapter of 1 Corinthians Paul writes just prior to this argument the following words of great comfort for all who have sinned:

> Or do you not know that the unrighteous shall not inherit the king-
> dom of God? Do not be deceived; neither fornicators, nor idolaters, nor
> adulterers, nor effeminate, nor homosexuals, nor thieves, nor the cov-
> etous, nor drunkards, nor revilers, nor swindlers, shall inherit the
> kingdom of God. And such were some of you; but you were washed,
> but you were sanctified, but you were justified in the name of the Lord
> Jesus Christ, and in the Spirit of our God (6: 9–11).

No, this is not the unpardonable sin. No matter how grievous our sins, we are justified—declared righteous before God—in the name of the Lord Jesus Christ. These are words of comfort, indeed.

But another question arises. Are not other sins within the body, and if so, are they not also as heinous as sexual sins? If a comparison is being made here between internal and external sins, as we have argued above, then drunkenness or drug abuse, for example, are surely within the body as well. Doesn't this make the observations above invalid? How are sexual sins really different?

That's a valid question. To understand the nature of sexual sin according to the Bible, we begin in chapter 4 an in-depth exegesis of these verses.

NOTES

1. "Ousted Radio Pastor to Join Calvary Chapel Staff," *Christianity Today,* February 8, 1993. The comment of Dr. David Hocking as reported in a news account.

2. David Neff, "Are All Sins Created Equal?", *Christianity Today,* 20 November 1987, 20–21.

3. Thomas Watson, *The Ten Commandments* (Carlisle, Pa.: Banner of Truth, 1692, reprinted 1965), 154.

4. Ibid., 153.

5. Ibid., 154.

6. Ibid., 158.

7. "Are All Sins Created Equal?" David Neff, Christianity Today, 20 November 1987, 20.

8. Watson, *The Ten Commandments*, 156.

9. Victor Hamilton, *The Book of Genesis, Chapters 1–17* (Grand Rapids, Mich.: Eerdmans, 1990), 179–180.

10. John Blanchard, *More Gathered Gold* (Welwyn, England: Evangelical Press, 1986), 294.

11. John Calvin, *Commentary on the Epistles of Paul the Apostle to the Corinthians, Volume 1* (Grand Rapids, Mich.: Eerdmans, 1979 reprint), 219–20.

12. C. K. Barrett, *The First Epistle to the Corinthians* (New York: Harper & Row, 1968), 150–51.

13. Thomas C. Edwards, *A Commentary on the First Epistle to the Corinthians* (Minneapolis, Minn.: Klock & Klock Christian Publishers, 1885, reprinted 1979), 149.

14. Ibid., 150.

15. R. C. H. Lenski, *The Interpretation of I and II Corinthians* (Minneapolis, Minn.: Augsburg, 1937), 267–68.

16. Ibid., 268.

CHAPTER FOUR

SEXUAL SIN: A BIBLICAL EXEGESIS

The doctrine of a minister must credit his life, and his life adorn his doctrine.

Jean Daille

*W*e have made a case for distinguishing sins within the body from those without. This raises the questions "Are not all sins against the body—be they drunkenness, drug abuse, or sexual sin—equally heinous? Why single out sexual sins?

How are sexual sins really different? That question has been considered by a number of prominent exegetes, and most agree that a comparison is plainly in view in Paul's words in 1 Corinthians 6:18: "Every other sin that a man commits is outside the body, but the immoral man sins against his own body." What the commentators argue, generally, is that sins such as drunkenness and drug abuse are sins against the body but not in the same way as sexual immorality. The uniqueness of sexual sin, to put it another way, is not in its degree of evil but rather in the direct way sexual sin strikes at the body and, through the body, at the whole human personality.

We will engage in some in-depth exegesis in this chapter so that we might understand the import of this key verse in recognizing sexual sin's consequences. In general many of the modern commentators go further than the interpretation advanced by John Calvin centuries ago. Calvin argues that sexual sin is above all other sin in its moral implications; many modern commentators add that Paul is arguing sexual sin affects the human body in a unique manner, and as some argue, removes the body which belongs to Christ and unites it to another person in a way that violates Christ, or the Spirit, most directly.[1]

TWO PREVAILING VIEWS

The exegetical difficulties presented by this text have been discussed for centuries. The major question seems to come down to this concern: What does "outside the body" mean here, especially since sexual immorality is singled out as being "against" the body of the one who sins in this manner?

Gordon Fee argues that the solutions come down to two. First, he sees the grammatical structure of the verse paralleling the structure of verses 12 and 13 earlier in the chapter, and that some will conclude that the apostle Paul is placing sin in a class of its own. Fee views the

> . . . first clause as a Corinthian slogan, which Paul then qualifies in the second clause, as [he had] in vv. 12–13. This would go something like: "All sin, whatever it is that a man commits, is outside the body," you say (or, you say?). "To the contrary, there is one sin in particular that is against one's own physical body, namely sexual immorality." There are several things in favor of this . . . . This is an attractive option, and may well be right. Nonetheless it is an abrupt word to follow the prohibition, that there was no immediate internal clues to suggest it, and the emphasis on "his own body" does not seem to respond to their slogan as such, which emphasizes the noncorporeal nature of all sin.[2]

In this first view, as argued by Calvin, Lenski, and others previously noted, sexual immorality is in a class by itself. Paul is not denying that several other sins have reference to the human body; instead he is saying what causes sexual sin to be "against the body" is that compared to other sins, it is in a class by itself.

The second option, Fee notes, is to see the phrase "outside the body" as a Pauline construct, formulated in the larger context of verses 13–20 and especially as a means of setting up by way of contrast the real concern, that "he who sins sexually sins against his own body." In this view the *de* ("but") points out the exception—it qualifies "every sin" to mean "every other sin" except the one spoken of in this clause. Paul's urgency is not with "other sins"; rather, he is arguing that "every other sin is apart from the body" in the sense that no other sin is directed specifically towards one's own body in the way that sexual immorality is. How so?

The answer lies with what has already been said in verses 15–17 and in light of what he will say about "one's own body" in 7:4. His concern is not with what affects and does not affect the body, but with the special character of sexual immorality and how that sin is directed especially against the body as "for the Lord." In fornicating with a prostitute a man removes his body (which is the temple of the Spirit, purchased by God and destined for resurrection) from union with Christ and makes it a member of her body, thereby putting it under her mastery (6:12b; compare with 7:4). Every other sin is apart from (i.e., not "in") the body in this singular sense.[3]

THE ARGUMENT IS SIMPLE. SEXUAL SIN ATTACKS THE BODY, AND IT HAS A SPECIAL SPIRITUAL EFFECT AGAINST THE BODY AND AGAINST THE REDEEMER OF THE BODY.

The second exegetical option is preferred by Fee and other modern commentators. This is confirmed by what follows in verses 19–20. The apostle could be said to reason as follows: "My body is not my own, if I am in Christ, for it is a temple of the Holy Spirit through redeeming grace. Any sexual sin is directed against the body and therefore against the place where God's Spirit resides."

The argument is simple. Sexual sin attacks the body, and it has a special spiritual effect against the body and against the Redeemer of the body. The evil is not greater, but the effect is devastating. Fee may get close to the significance of all of this, though his conclusion differs slightly from that of Calvin, Lenski, and the others quoted above, when he concludes, "Thus the unique nature of sexual sin is not so much that one sins against one's own self, but against one's own body as viewed in terms of its place in redemptive history."[4] In Fee's opinion it may well be true that one sins against one's own self in sexual immorality, but the point Paul is making here is that sexual sin is to be viewed eschatologically, specifically in terms of the ultimate purpose of the body's redemption in Christ.

Sexual union is the joining of all that one person is, in both body and soul, with all that another person is. It is the commitment of one's very being to the being of another person. It involves the commitment of one body to another in a way no other sin does. The Christian's body is the particular location of redemption and reconciliation (Philippians 3:12–23). It is the place where salvation and redemption will have the greatest demonstration of God's power. In adultery covenantal commitment is broken, and God's redemptive purpose for the whole person is repudiated in a most vile manner.

The only serious exegetical opposition, sometimes offered to the previously stated two views, seeks to view Paul's words as a counteractive move against a false slogan prominent in the context of the Corinthians. This interpretation, advocated by C.F.D. Moule, advanced the idea that the phrase was "a slogan of the Corinthian libertines, to which Paul replies with the assertion that fornication is not a deed committed outside the personality and in such a way as not to affect it, but is a sin against the body itself, and must therefore be avoided." The view, stated by a contemporary defender of it, goes as follows: "Every sin that a man commits is outside the body" is the slogan, and verse 18 offers the corrective word when Paul writes, "on the contrary the one who commits sexual immorality sins against his own body." Moule advanced this idea by writing that "By this slogan the Corinthians meant that the physical body had nothing to do with sin. The physical body was morally irrelevant, for sin took place on a completely different level of one's being. Paul responded by saying that the body was not morally irrelevant and that by committing sexual immorality one sinned against his own body."[5]

In this view the libertine slogan, it is said, argued that the body had nothing to do with sin, and thus in writing this portion of his epistle Paul is simply showing why this is not true.

C.K. Barrett counters the "slogan view" by writing,

> This attractive explanation is not entirely satisfying, because Paul's reply seems to accept the general proposition, and makes an exception to it (cf. verses 12f.), which leaves us with the original problem. It is perhaps best to suppose that Paul is writing rather loosely, and not in the manner of a textbook of moral philosophy. This interpretation goes back to Calvin.[6]

It would appear that this seemingly ingenious interpretation offers itself as compelling precisely because of the difficulties raised by this text. These difficulties, however, have been adequately addressed by the historic views of this text which have been advanced by Protestant scholars since Calvin.

Both Charles Hodge and Frederick Godet appear to simply summarize the correct understanding of the text and thereby underscore just how serious sexual immorality really is for the one who, in union with Christ, has received the Holy Spirit's indwelling presence. Hodge writes: ". . . [fornication] is altogether peculiar in its effects upon the body; not so much in its physical as in its moral and spiritual effects. The idea runs through the Bible that there is something mysterious in the commerce of the sexes, and in the effects which flow from it." Hodge then concludes this understanding's application by writing, "Every other sin, however degrading and ruinous to the health, even drunkenness, is external to the body, that is, external to its life. But fornication, involving as it does a community of life, is a sin against the body itself, incompatible, as the Apostle had just taught, with the design of its creation, and with its immortal destiny."[7]

Godet speaks of Paul uttering here "a cry of horror," and adds, "For a man to give to a degraded person a right over him by such a union, is not this to place himself in the most ignoble kind of dependence?"[8] I find myself in agreement with Godet, who wisely concludes, "I think it is better to seek to penetrate the depth of the apostolic thought than arbitrarily to recompose the text according to our own ideas."[9]

WHAT IS DISTRESSING IS HOW MODERN WRITERS SOMETIMES AVOID ETHICAL IMPLICATIONS IN A TEXT LIKE THIS BY ADVANCING THE "SLOGAN VIEW." . . . THEY NEED TO BETTER ADDRESS REAL ETHICAL ISSUES IN TERMS OF THE SEXUALLY IMMORAL PASTOR.

What is distressing is how modern writers sometimes avoid ethical implications in a text like this by advancing the "slogan view." This kind of approach is honest scholarship, but the conclusions often drawn from it need to better address real ethical issues in terms of the sexually immoral pastor. Writes one modern exegete who ably defends the "slogan view":

> Sexual immorality is denounced repeatedly and vigorously throughout Scripture. Sexual immorality is a serious offense but it is questionable whether severity alone automatically demands permanent disqualification, for sexual immorality is not an unpardonable sin. Moreover, in 1 Timothy 1:15 Paul himself claimed to be the foremost of sinners (cf. Rom. 7:24), and yet elsewhere he defended his right to be an apostle (1 Cor. 9:1–2; 2 Cor. 11:5; 12:11–12).[10]

In response to this argument, let's remember that no one seriously argues that a particular sin, such as sexual immorality, is unpardonable. Further, it is valid to ask whether any sin is of such a nature that it can weigh upon the issue of restoration to pastoral office. If a sin against one's own body is not relevant—and thus a real possibility for some kind of disqualification from office—then what is? What, exactly, does Paul's claim concerning his previous life as an infidel and a God-hater have to do directly with the subject of pastors' sexual misconduct? Present day pastors, in most traditions, are called by local congregations who must examine their lives for the character of a man who must remain an example to their flock (see 1 Timothy 3:1–8).

I do not think the argument regarding the restoration of a sexually fallen pastor to public pastoral ministry has anything to do with Paul's lifestyle before his conversion. (We shall consider other significantly related matters in ensuing chapters, but here we are merely considering the ethical significance of an important passage like 1 Corinthians 6:18–20.)

In conclusion, the historic and traditional Protestant understanding of this text best fits the evidence of both the context and the theological/ethical teaching of the New Testament. Sexual immorality is an immense sin, one with even greater implications than other sins that affect the life of the individual believer and the church community. Paul's conclusion to this section of correspondence is summarized in verses 18–20. He urges believers to take every precaution to flee from all sexual immorality. In a situation like that in ancient Corinth this mindset would be important to cultivate because of the sexually permissive climate that existed. In order to make his point he contrasts the effects of sexual sin with other sins such as drunkenness and gluttony, showing that these sins also affect the body, but only when committed in excess. Sexual sin has a unique sinfulness in itself. It is sin against one's inner personality.

This is most likely what Paul envisions in verse 18 when he makes the second reference to the "body." Adds the *Bible Study Commentary,* a frequently helpful summarizing guide, "It should cause little wonder that the sexually promiscuous person actually destroys his own personality. Such a result is inherent in the nature of the sin."[11]

Make no mistake about it, sexual immorality is a great sin because it is uniquely sin against one's own body, and thus it is a sin with profound emotional, spiritual and eschatological implications, regardless of the precise view taken of this most important text.

PASTORAL ADULTERY: AN EVEN GREATER SIN

It is my thesis that adultery by pastors, which has reached epidemic proportions in the contemporary church, is an even *greater* sin than adultery in general. Why?

Some sins are more damaging than others precisely because of who it is that commits them. This observation is both logical and biblical.

James 3:1 reasons that not many should aspire to teaching the Word of God to the church, "knowing that as such we shall incur a stricter judgment (or greater condemnation)." Pastors shall receive stricter judgment. Why? Because the teaching they render to the church, in both doctrine and life, affects so many others. This seems to be precisely why Paul reasons elsewhere that the man of God (his term for the overseer/pastor) must carefully guard both his life and doctrinal teaching. The two may never be separated. He counsels Timothy: "Pay close attention to yourself and to your teaching; persevere in these things; for as you do this you will insure salvation both for yourself and for those who hear you" (1 Timothy 4:16). When a man ceases to watch his life and his teaching (the two must never be separated as we often do in our age), he jeopardizes his own soul and the souls of all those who hear him. Can there be any doubt that this man holds within himself great potential for praise, and even greater potential for condemnation?

The *Westminster Larger Catechism,* a standard that has exercised considerable positive influence over the life of the church in the West for centuries, states this principle plainly. It is one rarely expressed, and even more rarely understood, in our age of relativism. The *Catechism* says:

> **Question 150.** Are all transgressions of the law of God equally heinous in themselves, and in the sight of God?
> **Answer.** All transgressions of the law of God are not equally heinous; but some sins in themselves and by reason of several aggravations are more heinous in the sight of God than others (Cf. John 19:11; Ezk. 8:6, 13, 15; 1 John 5:16; Psalm 78:17, 32, 56).

Question 151. What are those aggravations that make some sins more heinous than others?

Answer. 1. From the persons offending; if they be of riper age, greater experience of grace eminent for profession, gifts, place, office, guides to others, and whose example is likely to be followed by others. 2. From the parties offended; if immediately against God, his attributes and worship; against Christ, and his grace; the Holy Spirit, his witness, and workings; against superiors, men of eminency, and such as we stand especially related and engaged unto; against any of the saints, particularly weak brethren, the souls of them, or any other, and the common good of all or many. 3. From the nature and quality of the offense; if it be against the express letter of the law, break many commandments, contain in it many sins; if not only conceived in the heart, but breaks forth in words and actions, scandalize others, and admit of no reparation; if against means, mercies, judgments, light of nature, conviction of conscience, public or private admonitions, censures of the church, civil punishments; and our prayers, purposes, promises, vows, covenants, and engagements to God or men. . . . 4. From circumstances of time and place . . . if in public, or in the presence of others, who are thereby likely to be provoked or defiled.[12]

Though not infallible, this 350-year-old guide certainly expresses the way the Westminster divines understood some of the very questions before us in this book. What is to be observed here is the clear way these Protestant theologians treated sins. There should be no doubt that sexual sin is heinous, and that sexual sin in a pastor is even more heinous, regardless of what view one takes of certain exegetical particularities that we now are exploring.

Pastors who commit adultery put their own bodies into an illicit sexual union that compromises their past ordination (i.e., "the laying on of hands") before the church body, makes their vows to be faithful to their ministry meaningless, and scandalizes their entire congregation, especially those new and weak in the faith. Their sin becomes a grievous public assault upon the nuptial image of Christ (the groom) and the church (His bride), because the pastor is called upon to be a role model of purity as an undershepherd in service to the Bridegroom Himself.

No Christian belongs to himself. He is the Lord's, as 1 Corinthians 6:19b–20 reasons ". . . you are not your own[.] For you have been bought with a price: therefore glorify God in your body." Surely if no Christian belongs to himself, no pastor belongs to himself regarding both his giftedness and his calling to minister to the church as an overseer of the flock. The fundamental nature of all pastoral ministry is stewardship: we are not our own; we have been given by Christ to His church (cf. Ephesians 4:7–13), and our task is to serve the church by both life and teaching. If we give ourselves to sin of the type that shatters our stewardship and threatens to scandalize the very flock over which the Holy Spirit has made us overseers, we may find ourselves disqualified from ever rendering effective pastoral ministry to the church again.

Why is this so difficult to understand in our day? In other times in the history of the church the great number of those who counseled and taught the church had a different consensus (see chapter 7) than that of our generation. What has happened? Could it be we have both a low view of sin, as well as a low view of the lifestyle expected of the pastor?

NOTES

1. Jay E. Smith, "Can Fallen Leaders Be Restored to Leadership?", *Bibliotheca Sacra* 151 (October–December 1994): 471.

2. Gordon D. Fee, *The First Epistle to the Corinthians,* (Grand Rapids, Mich.: Eerdmans, 1987), 262.

3. Ibid., 263.

4. Ibid., 263.

5. As quoted in Jay E. Smith, "Can Fallen Leaders Be Restored," 473–74.

6. C. K. Barrett, *The First Epistle to the Corinthians* (New York: Harper & Row, 1968), 150.

7. Charles Hodge, *Commentary on the First Epistle to the Corinthians* (Grand Rapids, Mich.: Eerdmans, 1969 reprint), 105–6.

8. Frederick L. Godet, *The First Epistle to the Corinthians* (Grand Rapids, Mich.: Zondervan, 1886, 1971 reprint), 311.

9. Ibid., 310.

10. Jay E. Smith, "Can Fallen Leaders," 477–78.

11. Curtis Vaughan and Thomas D. Lea, *Bible Study Commentary: 1 Corinthians* (Grand Rapids, Mich.: Zondervan, 1983), 66.

12. Westminster Confession of Faith and The Larger and Shorter Catechisms, adopted by delegates at the Westminster Assembly, London, 1643-47.

CHAPTER FIVE

IS HE QUALIFIED?

Is that man likely to do much good, or fit to be a minister of Christ, that will speak for Him an hour, and by his life will preach against Him all the week beside?

Richard Baxter

Sexual harassment, sexual abuse, sexual misconduct, child abuse, moral failure. Each phrase has appeared in a growing number of documents drafted and discussed by denominations and church agencies. As concern for this problem increases and as the problem becomes widely known, subjects once never discussed openly are now on the front pages of both secular and religious press.

Nearly everyone knows at least one pastor who has fallen. And most have read of many others. The public scandals of Jim Bakker and Jimmy Swaggart are now a sad part of our history, but the growing tragedy of thousands of men who are falling weekly is not so widely known, or immediately apparent. As one writer notes in the Canadian evangelical magazine *Faith Today,* the movement to draft documents to deal with the problem is widespread and fundamental:

> Some of the documents are 30-page tomes; others are one-page codes. Some deal only with clergy abuse; others apply to anyone in leader-

ship. Some are replete with legal terminology, others with Scripture quotations. But the over-riding concern is the same—the moral and ethical integrity of Christian leadership.[1]

Integrity, both ethically and morally, is the issue that church and denominational leaders must address if we would come to some understanding of the problem of pastoral sexual misconduct and the related question of restoration to pastoral office.

THE BASIS FOR PASTORAL QUALIFICATION

It is hard to imagine that we have come to a time in our collective ecclesiastical experience when we must actually advance arguments proving a man must be qualified before he holds pastoral office. That, however, is the case.

Every Christian has both the right and responsibility to use every possible opportunity to disseminate the gospel, but not all are called to the pastoral ministry. This is generally not recognized as it should be in our day.

When the apostle Peter wrote, "Shepherd the flock of God among you, exercising oversight not under compulsion, but voluntarily, according to the will of God" (1 Peter 5:2), he was addressing a selected and recognized few who oversee the church of God through the ministry of the Word. Those men were the elders, or pastors, of the flock of God. They had been chosen by a church for the explicit purpose of giving themselves to this work; today the church still selects its pastors, though the manner has changed over the ages. The fact that the process of our selecting pastors is less obvious today tells us how far we have fallen from the Scriptures and the holy traditions of the Christian faith.

Simply put, all are not to labor in word and doctrine in the office of pastor. It was with this idea in mind that Paul clearly instructed Timothy when he wrote:

Do not neglect the spiritual gift within you, which was bestowed upon you through prophetic utterance with the laying on of hands by the presbytery. Take pains with these things; be absorbed in them, so that your progress may be evident to all. Pay close attention to yourself and to your teaching; persevere in these things; for as you do this you will insure salvation both for yourself and for those who hear you (1 Timothy 4:14–16).

Before the day of recent "lay renewal movements" (which have proper and improper concerns) we did not seriously doubt that a man must be called of God, qualified both doctrinally and morally, and accepted formally by the church. All of this was clearly required before the pastor entered ministry. C.H. Spurgeon, certainly not the proponent of a high-church ecclesiastical tradition, and one who was not himself formally ordained, wrote: "He that can toy with his ministry and count it to be like a trade, or like any other profession, was never called of God. But he that has a charge pressing on his heart, and a woe ringing in his ear, and preaches as though he heard the cries of hell behind him, and saw his God looking down on him—oh, how that man entreats the Lord that his hearers may not hear in vain!"[2]

WHAT HAS BEEN CONSISTENTLY TRUE [OF THE OFFICE OF CHURCH ELDER (OVERSEER/PASTOR) AND DEACON] . . . IS THAT BOTH REQUIRE THAT A PERSON BE EXAMINED IN SOME MANNER AND BE PROVEN QUALIFIED BEFORE ENTERING THE OFFICE.

Paul urges Timothy to "make full proof of [his] ministry" (2 Timothy 4:5, AV), which implies fulfilling the proof he had already given at some previous point. Paul urges, on another occasion, that a brother, Archippus, should "Take heed to the ministry that you have received in the Lord, that you may fulfill it" (Colossians 4:17). Archippus was being told to fulfill the stewardship of what had been entrusted to him in his call. If the elder "must be above reproach as God's steward" (Titus 1:7), then it makes sense that he has been granted authority following an examination of his life and a subsequent entrusting with the stewardship of the mysteries of the gospel.

The New Testament describes two office bearers, or servant leadership roles: the church elder *(overseer* and *pastor* are synonyms) and the deacon. Traditionally, the nature of these offices, the manner of choosing those who hold them, the work they are to actually render to the church, and the preparation required before entering office have all been approached differently. What has been consistently true, however, is that *both require that a person be examined in some manner and proven qualified before entering the office.*

The pastor is an overseer, which describes the principal focus of his labors on behalf of the church. He "looks out over the flock" guarding, feeding, and serving it with his very life. His authority is not in his charm or intellect, his powerful personality, or even in his spiritual gifts. His authority is in the gospel of Christ, which he carefully and properly uses to serve the people of God through preaching in public and in private, or as the apostle taught fellow church leaders, "teaching you publicly and from house to house" (Acts 20:20). The pastor is to "exhort in sound doctrine and to refute those who contradict" (Titus 1:9).

ALL OF THIS REQUIRES THAT [THE PASTOR] BE MORE THAN THE ORDINARY CHRISTIAN MAN. HE IS CALLED, BY IMPLICATION, THE "MAN OF GOD" IN THE PASTORAL EPISTLES.

He does all this in order to fulfill his ministerial calling. He is called, further, to guard the spiritual well-being of his people through sober counsel and earnest prayer (James 5:14–15). Simply put, he is a shepherd, serving under his Master; therefore he continually lays down his life for the sheep "night and day . . . with tears" (Acts 20:31).

All of this requires that he be more than the ordinary Christian man. He is called, by implication, the "man of God" in the pastoral epistles. He is a man who has been carefully examined and found ready to serve the church. As Paul says in the passage we shall shortly look at more carefully, "An overseer, then, must be . . . must be . . . must be . . ." Over and over he makes it plain that what is desirable in all mature Christian men is an absolute must for the pastor who would be qualified to serve the flock.

Because the pastor will comfort, rebuke, lead, and love the Christian church as a family, he must have the qualities of a good and kind father (1 Timothy 3:5). Because he will, as a shepherd, guide the sheep through leading and feeding them (1 Peter 5:2; Acts 20:28), he must be proven capable to serve in this capacity. And, because he will nurture the flock through his administration of the ordinances (i.e., communion and baptism), and because his influence in every matter touches the life of the church, and because he remains an example before the church, he must be qualified to hold the office of elder. He must be "the man of God" before the congregation (1 Timothy 6:11; 2 Timothy 3:17).

PASTOR VERSUS PRIEST

It has been argued sometimes that the office of New Testament pastor parallels the Old Testament office of priest. This is not true, strictly speaking, for the theological equivalent of the Old Testament priesthood is found in our High Priest, the Lord Jesus Christ, who alone fulfills the type by being in Himself "without blemish" (Hebrews 2:17; 3:1; 4:14–15; 8:1; 9:7, 11; 10:11, 21). All the Old Testament requirements for ceremonial purity are fulfilled in Him alone. Furthermore, all believers now make up a kingdom of priests who have become a universal and holy Christian priesthood (1 Peter 2: 5, 9).

One writer notes that the relationship of the priest to the pastor

is not precise. Restrictions placed on priests reflect concerns for ceremonial cleanness in ways unparalleled in the New Testament. Also as mediators between God and the people, the priests revealed God's holy character in a way that today's elders do not. So directly applying the

standards of the Old Testament priesthood to the office of elder is pre-
carious, as illustrated from the requirement that the priest must be
free from physical defect (Leviticus 21:16–20).[3]

These Old Testament prescriptions of ceremonial cleanness in those who led the worship of the congregation in the
wilderness have their fulfillment in the One who perfectly kept
the whole Law for us, our Lord Jesus Christ. Directly applying
them to pastors under the New Covenant is not theologically
warranted. It is true, however, that Christ, the Chief Shepherd
of the flock of God, as a result of His redemptive work, gives
men (cf. Ephesians 4: 7–11) to serve His flock, and these men
must be qualified to model the gospel. The apostle Paul declares (Ephesians 4:11) that certain individuals have been set
apart for the church by Christ's priestly sacrifice and labor.

Under the Old Covenant, God declared that He would give to
Israel pastors, or shepherds (Jeremiah 3:15). Those shepherds
were enabled to speak with earnestness and unction. They did
this precisely because their lives displayed an obvious holiness of
the Lord. God called those men "watchmen" (Jeremiah 23:4).
They were put in place to warn, plead, and direct, and the shepherds' actions were to conform to their message in every way,
or their message could simply not be heard by Israel.

If the lives of New Covenant pastors do not measure up to
a standard of moral purity that consistently "gives no offense
either to Jews or to Greeks or to the church of God" (1 Corinthians 10:32), then the same results will occur as under the
Old Covenant: the people will see in this man a model that
compromises the purity of the Savior. When this happens under the New Covenant the ethical and moral consequences are
just as great, if not greater, than those under the Old. God,
who is the same holy being, is exercised about His people having
holy examples–shepherds, prophets (preachers), watchmen, and
"men of God"–who reflect His purity and His holiness.

It is because of all of this that some have improperly argued for a direct relationship between the priests, and their
requirement for ceremonial cleanness, and the office of elder
under the New Covenant. The exegesis of this argument is

wrong, and the conclusions are thus debatable at certain points, but the concern expressed is in harmony with the New Covenant.

THE QUALIFICATIONS GOD REQUIRES

The biblical qualifications for pastors are given clearly in the New Testament. The great preacher and expositor C. H. Spurgeon believed every pastor and would-be pastor must examine his own qualifications:

> When I think upon the all but infinite mischief which may result from a mistake as to our vocation for the Christian pastorate, I feel overwhelmed with fear lest any of us should be slack in examining our credentials; and I had rather that we stood too much in doubt, and examined too frequently, than that we should become cumberers of the ground. There are not lacking many exact methods by which a man may test his call to the ministry if he earnestly desires to do so. It is imperative upon him not to enter the ministry until he has made solemn quest and trial of himself as to this point. His own personal salvation being secure, he must investigate as to the further matter of his call to office; the first is vital to himself as a Christian, the second equally vital to him as a pastor.[4]

Being Willing to Ask About Qualifications

Most church leaders agree that the Scripture does speak to the matter of "qualifications"; yet it is astounding how often this is treated with a response akin to a shrug of the shoulders, downplaying or ignoring questions of moral and spiritual credentials. I have, for instance, watched those "shoulder shrugs" while participating on various church councils that examine men before ordination. Such meetings convene in order to recommend whether the man is a fit person for the office of pastor. We look at both his grasp of doctrinal Christianity and his own conversion, his growth, and present lifestyle. After some hours of discussion with the man the council will meet in private to discuss the next step. "Should we proceed? Or should we tell the man that we think he is not ready to take on the responsibilities inherent in the pastoral office?" Those two questions comprise an important decision regarding a potential shepherd of God's flock in the local church.

Some years ago I was asked to chair a committee for my evangelical denomination where the duties included pre-examining men for ordination before the council was convened. In our polity the committee of pastors did not ordain; the local church had that authority. Our job was to test, to question, and then to recommend. We examined a good number of men each year. More than half of them were unprepared in my own view—doctrinally and/or personally. Several times we recommended that the church not ordain the man.

Often the local church ignored our counsel and proceeded without our approval, finally ordaining the man at a later date. What was particularly troubling was how infrequently the man or his local church bothered to inquire as to our reasons. This eventually precipitated a crisis of conscience and led to my resignation from this pre-ordination committee.

IN ALL MY YEARS OF SERVICE ON COUNCILS AND COMMITTEES I HAVE RARELY HEARD A CANDIDATE ASKED: "WHAT ABOUT YOUR LIFE MORALLY?". . . . WE SIMPLY DO NOT PROBE THE ISSUE OF PROVEN CHARACTER AND PERSONAL PURITY VERY DEEPLY.

In all my years of service on councils and committees I have rarely heard a candidate asked: "What about your life morally?" We might discuss the man's marriage, and that often in a rather shallow manner. Almost never did I hear the candidate asked, "Are you sexually pure, at this time, before God?" Or, "Have you so lived, as you have prepared yourself for ministry over the years, that your life is 'above reproach' right now as you stand before us a candidate for office?" We simply do not probe the issue of proven character and personal purity very deeply.

In an age where sexual misconduct is common, both in the culture and in the church at large, I am compelled to ask,

"Why do we never ask these kinds of questions before we ordain a man?" We live in a time where the statistics suggest that habits in the church are not that different from those in the general population. Should we not be more concerned that we both help people in this area, as well as preserve the pastoral office from men who are not qualified for ministry? Should churches not be more concerned to do background checks on men they call to be their pastors?

In these professional examination procedures we may ask a dozen doctrinally oriented questions, for every one ethical and moral question. I am not demeaning doctrinal questions, for far too many pastors are fuzzy and unclear in this area as well, but why do we almost totally ignore the areas of sex, money, and power? Is it not in these areas that most of the ethical and moral failures will surface?

Matters of Personal Integrity and Character

In 1 Timothy 3:2–7, almost every requirement listed has to do with personal integrity and proven character. Read carefully the requirements Paul gives:

> An overseer [i.e. pastor], then, must be above reproach, the husband of one wife, temperate, prudent, respectable, hospitable, able to teach, not addicted to wine, or pugnacious, but gentle, uncontentious, free from the love of money. He must be one who manages his own household well, keeping his children under control with all dignity (but if a man does not know how to manage his own household, how will he take care of the church of God?); and not a new convert, lest he become conceited and fall under the condemnation incurred by the devil. And he must have a good reputation with those outside the church, so that he may not fall into reproach and the snare of the devil.

In a parallel manner the apostle gives to Titus similar personal requirements for the one who would be a pastor when he writes:

> . . . if any man be above reproach, the husband of one wife, having children who believe, not accused of dissipation or rebellion. For the overseer must be above reproach as God's steward, not self-willed, not

quick tempered, not addicted to wine, not pugnacious, not fond of sordid gain, but hospitable, loving what is good, sensible, just, devout, self-controlled, holding fast the faithful word which is in accordance with the teaching, that he may be able to exhort in sound doctrine and to refute those who contradict (Titus 1:6–9).

These two passages are the *locus classicus* of the New Testament on pastoral qualification. The important qualifications regarding the man's sexual purity are found in three phrases that literally jump out at us. These are: (1) "above reproach and blameless"; (2) "the husband of one wife"; and (3) "a good reputation with those outside the church." We need to carefully consider each of these important qualifying requirements for pastoral ministry.

The eligibility of a man to continue in pastoral ministry, having once been placed in office after careful examination and proper qualification, must ultimately hinge upon the written Scripture. Decisions regarding qualifications for pastoral ministry must not be determined by our emotions, nor arbitrarily or democratically, but by "every word that proceeds out of the mouth of God" (Matthew 4:4). If we will not use the Scriptures as the source of all truth for faith and practice, then we shall never be able to respond adequately to vexing issues that threaten to overrun us in this day. Let's look at three phrases that deal with sexual purity in the pastorate.

"Above Reproach and Blameless"

The requirements that the minister be "above reproach and blameless" clearly are concerned with moral purity. The phrase "above reproach" comes from a compound Greek word that means "unimpeachable" or "unassailable." The word "blameless" comes from another word that seems to have a similar meaning in Paul's use in both 1 Timothy 3:2 and Titus 1:7. The wording in the two texts is quite close in the Greek, and thus the terms should be treated as virtual synonyms.

The *New American Commentary* says of the word *blameless,* "It may serve as a general, covering term for the following list of virtues that should distinguish a church leader. The etymology of the word suggests the meaning not to be taken hold of. It describes a person of such character that no one can properly bring against him a charge of unfitness."[5] Gordon Fee believes that the reference, consistent with the list of words that follows, is to observable behavior. With other commentators he suggests that the term is an all-embracing moral one.[6]

The term "above reproach" is used elsewhere in 1 Timothy 5:7 and 6:14. In the first reference the word is used to describe how children are to care for their parents "so that they may be above reproach." In 6:14 the word is used with a Greek word which means "spotless" or "without blemish" in telling Timothy to "keep the commandment without stain or reproach until the appearing of our Lord Jesus Christ." Extrabiblical evidence supports these definitions as well.

It is logical to understand that what is in view here is *present* status. The man might very well have been blameless in the past, or he might become blameless in the future, but the qualification of *this* verse is clear—he is blameless *now.*

CHARACTER IS NOT SET IN CEMENT. . . . PROGRESSIVE SANCTIFICATION MEANS EVEN THE WORST OF SINNERS CAN MAKE PROGRESS.

Every other mention of this idea in the pastoral epistles leads to the same conclusion. When we go further in 1 Timothy 3 we find a similar idea in the qualifications for those who would be deacons. Paul says: "And let these also first be tested; then let them serve as deacons if they are beyond reproach" (3:10). The fact, further, that the elder "must not be a recent convert" (3:6) also implies that some time must pass so that the man's present life can be evaluated so that it can be seen that he is "above reproach" or "blameless." This may well be why Paul says in 5:22, "Do not lay hands upon anyone too hastily," as this would also involve a violation of the requirement to be "above reproach."

Does past sexual failure automatically keep a person out of pastoral ministry? If a man has been sexually immoral, living the lifestyle of an adulterer or fornicator, must he forego consideration of pastoral ministry? These texts do not support an affirmative answer. Let me explain.

Character is not set in cement. It is, thankfully, not immutable in this life. Past sins might well influence one's present life, as is obvious from the devastation that some sins bring to the body alone, but they need not do so in all circumstances. Progressive sanctification means even the worst of sinners can make progress.

This prompts one writer to say, "There seems to be no reason why the sexual offender, who confesses his sin, repents, and then consistently shows evidence of a blameless character, cannot meet the requirement of being blameless or above reproach. The past violation of the standard does not automatically preclude its future attainment."[7]

CERTAIN SINS, EVEN COMMITTED IN THE LIVES OF UNBELIEVERS BEFORE CONVERSION, DO HAVE AN ENDURING EFFECT THAT WILL NEVER LEAVE A PERSON FOR A LIFETIME. THE EFFECT OF SUCH SINS MIGHT VERY WELL KEEP HIM FROM PROPERLY HOLDING THE OFFICE OF ELDER AND MINISTERING AS A PASTOR.

But before we jump on the bandwagon of a conclusion like this I would caution: Certain sins, even committed in the lives of unbelievers before conversion, do have an enduring effect that will never leave a person for a lifetime. The effect of such sins might very well keep him from properly holding the office of elder and ministering as a pastor in a local church. Let me illustrate with several fairly clear examples.

A man has a criminal record as a pedophile, seeking and abusing children. He truly repents, and the resultant lifestyle of many years afterward proves him to be a good and godly Christian man. Is he "above reproach" in terms of the requirement of this text? I seriously doubt it, due to the nature of his past sin and the effects this past would have upon service he would seek to render to the whole church. Parents of young children would naturally have a hard time trusting this man with ministry to their children.

Let's say a man has been divorced several times. His life for years had been profligate and wild, but now he's been a believer for a decade. He is well taught, a gifted teacher, and a faithful man to his present wife. Should he enter the pastoral ministry? I doubt it, for the same reason.

In every case wisdom will be needed. The Bible doesn't give us a checklist for being "above reproach." The words that follow help explain what is meant here, but we can't simply go down the list and say, "Well, he hasn't done this for three years, and he has positively been this way for four years, so now he is clearly 'above reproach' and we can make him a pastor."

To be qualified for pastoral ministry a man must have an unassailable moral reputation. I will come back to this observation later but for now this conclusion is plain in the light of the words that Paul uses and the context in which they occur.

"The Husband of One Wife"

In 1 Timothy 3:2 and Titus 1:6 Paul indicates that the pastor must be "the husband of one wife." This phrase has led to several interpretations that are worth mentioning. One is that this is a requirement for church leaders. This would mean that all elders must be married. In the light of 1 Corinthians 7:7–8, where Paul himself appears to have been a single man in ministry, and 1 Corinthians 7:1, and 32–35, where singleness is seen as a preferred state for effective ministry, this view seems to be unlikely. I believe it is more likely that Paul is assuming most men who would be pastors are already married; thus this is the proper context in which they must be examined to determine if they are qualified for ministry. Again we would note that determining a man's qualification for ministry is the issue at stake here.

A second view says Paul intends that the elder must not be a practicing polygamist, i.e., he must have only one wife. The translation of the popular NIV seems to favor this view to some extent when it reads "the husband of but one wife." One of the significant problems with this view is that polygamy was simply not a major problem in the society of Paul's time.

A third view sees this as a prohibition of remarriage, under all circumstances. Alfred Plummer, a very good exegete, defends this view by writing,

> A second marriage, although perfectly lawful and in some cases advisable, was so far a sign of weakness; a double family would in many cases be a serious hindrance to work. The Church could not afford to enlist any but its strongest men among its officers; and its officers must not be hampered more than other men with domestic cares.[8]

The strongest argument for this view is in the requirement for enrolled widows in 1 Timothy 5:9 where the same phrase in Greek has the meaning, quite literally, of one person only, and that in this lifetime.

In light of concern for domestic affairs being managed well, which is plainly in view in 1 Timothy 3:2, this third view seems without clear warrant in the larger context. It is an interpretation that doesn't work well in the larger context of what is in view in the character questions associated with the process of qualifying an elder.

A more common view, associated with the above in a different manner, says that Paul forbids a divorced man from ever holding the pastoral office. This view, often taken by conservative churches, Christian agencies and mission boards and societies, may have some practical reasons to defend it, but the New Testament will not permit it. (This view, by the way, is usually extended to include men who are married to wives who were previously divorced. It is also common to find churches that forbid such from teaching a Sunday school class, serving on certain committees, etc.)

I think the *New American Commentary* puts this view in the proper biblical light when it says:

> Another interpretation is to understand Paul to have prohibited a divorced man from serving as a church leader. While this can be Paul's meaning, the language is too general in its statement to make this interpretation certain. Some evangelical New Testament scholars suggest that there are New Testament passages that appear to permit divorce (Matthew 19:9; 1 Corinthians 7:15).[9]

Though some variation of the above third view might have merit, I believe the fourth is better grammatically, biblically, and logically.

This fourth view holds that "husband of one wife" is perhaps better translated "one-woman man." This view emphasizes the character of the man who is being considered and seeks to determine if he is qualified in terms of his actual moral character. The *New American Commentary* is again helpful when it says:

> It is better to see Paul having demanded that the church leader be faithful to his one wife. The Greek describes the overseer literally as a "one-woman kind of man" (cf. "faithful to his one wife," NEB). Lenski suggests that the term describes a man "who cannot be taken hold of on the score of sexual promiscuity or laxity. . . . Had Paul clearly meant to prohibit divorce, he could have said it unmistakably by using the Greek word for divorce (*apolyo*, Matt. 1:19).[10]

William Hendriksen concurs when he writes, "Accordingly, the meaning of our present passage is simply this, that an overseer or elder must be a man of unquestioned morality, one who is entirely true and faithful to his one and only wife; one who, being married, does not in pagan fashion enter into an immoral relationship with another woman."[11]

"A Good Reputation with Those Outside"

A third qualification for the pastor is to be well-respected by those who are outside of the church, that is, by non-Christians. This requirement, often ignored and frequently misunderstood, has some extremely important bearing on the question of restoring sexually immoral pastors to office, as we will also see later. For now we need to briefly consider this qualification for those who would enter the office of elder.

The "good reputation" is literally a "good witness." As with a credible witness in the court, who is completely believable because of his life before others, so this man has both a good name and good standing in the surrounding community. Says the *New American Commentary:* "The mention of the leader's name should not cause derision among the opponents of the gospel. The behavior of the leader should provide an example of integrity and commitment to the gospel he professes."[12]

The point is quite clear: If the overseer has an unsavory reputation with the unsaved world around the church, then the leader, and with him the entire church, will fall into disgrace. If the pastor has lived in such a manner as to cause unsaved people not to hear his message, then the devil has lured both the leader and his flock into a trap, for as Paul writes, "he may fall into reproach and the snare of the devil" (v. 7). This thought is stated well in the Weymouth translation: "It is needful also that he bear a good character with people outside the Church, lest he fall into reproach or a snare of the devil." As Lea and Griffin note in *the New American Commentary,*

> Christians must realize that unbelievers scrutinize their actions with a searchlight of fault-finding investigation. Paul's implied appeal is that church leaders give no opportunity for unbelievers genuinely to find fault. . . . In this verse Paul presented Satan as a hunter who lays out traps into which the careless, short-sighted Christian can fall.[13]

It is true that a man may be forgiven immediately of any sin, but it is not true that the effects of his sin will go unnoticed by the world. Character, which produces reputation in general, is essential for ministry. Abraham Lincoln put this relationship well when he said, "Character is like a tree and reputation its shadow. The shadow is what we think of it; the tree is the real thing."

Character can be rebuilt in many cases, but reputation may be destroyed in some cases, as numerous examples will prove. It seems that this is in view in Proverbs 6:32–33 where we read: "The one who commits adultery with a woman is lacking sense; He who would destroy himself does it. Wounds and disgrace he will find, and his reproach will not be blotted out."

> *THE WORLD WILL TEND TO EVALUATE ALL OF US BY OUR LEADERS. IF THEIR CONDUCT DISCREDITS OUR CORPORATE MESSAGE THEN THE WORLD SCOFFS, WITH A CERTAIN MEASURE OF JUSTICE. . .*

As we will see, all of this raises some major problems regarding restoring a sexually fallen pastor to office when he has abused his office and the very people he was called to protect. When this happens the children of darkness are often wiser than the children of light in recognizing that the man's reputation is seriously flawed and thus what he now seeks to do —mainly, develop good and godly character in others through the ministry of the Word—will not be acceptable.

Maintaining a proper reputation with those outside the faith is an often stated concern of the apostle Paul. (See 1 Corinthians 10:32; Philippians 2:15; Colossians 4:5; 1 Thessalonians 4:12; 1 Timothy 2:2; 5:14; 6:1; Titus 2:5, 8, 10; and 3:1–2.) It is expressed by others (Acts 22:12) and is a personal concern of the apostle Peter as well (1 Peter 2:12, 15; 3:1, 16). What is true for all believers is particularly true for would-be leaders. The world will tend to evaluate all of us by our leaders. If their conduct discredits our corporate message then the world scoffs, with a certain measure of justice, I might add, and the devil has successfully set his trap and brought about great destruction.

We must note that this qualification of a good reputation is quite subjective. The answer to the question "What do those outside the church think about this man's character?" will surely fluctuate from person to person and occasion to occasion. And we must not be quick to take every opposing word uttered against a pastor by some worldly people. But it must be observed that this requirement is nonetheless given to the church for a clearly stated purpose. We must be careful and wise in examining leaders in order that we not give the devil the tools with which he will set a trap that will destroy Christ's work in a particular church.

When basic requirements of character are missing in a man's lifestyle the world will notice, and his work will be discredited. This seems obvious, even to the point of being almost completely self-evident. But when we consider pastoral candidates, those character requirements are often ignored or downplayed.

A PROPER STANDARD

John Newton, author of the world's best known Christian hymn "Amazing Grace," was an eminent minister of the Church of England in the eighteenth century. He once remarked,

> None but he who made the world can make a Minister of the Gospel . . . . If a young man has capacity, [then] culture and application may make him a scholar, a philosopher, or an orator; but a true Minister must have certain principles, motives, feelings, and aims, which no industry or endeavors of men can either acquire or communicate. They must be given from above, or they cannot be received."[14]

The apostle Paul himself was overwhelmed with his own unfitness for the task. It was he who wrote, "for who is adequate for these things?" (2 Corinthians 2:16) when he sensed his own insufficiency. What is particularly troubling in our time is how infrequently one hears these sentiments. We have the best-trained, at least professionally, and most highly esteemed pastors in memory. With it has come a measure of confidence that is astounding. Even in the 1800s one commentator noted that the American pastor was being called "the most 'able Minister of the New Testament' that the Church has ever known."[15]

We must be careful, when we consider qualifications for the ministry of the gospel, never to lower, elevate, or deviate from the divine pattern. It has been obvious to the church for centuries that not all the requirements for pastoral ministry are of equal importance. Some qualifications, such as the ability to speak in all circumstances in a manner that is particularly polished, or the lack of a finely cultivated mind in intellectual matters, may hinder the progress of pastoral labor, but these do not necessarily keep the man from the office. The absence of other qualifications, however—solid character and moral strength—will inevitably destroy the very reputation of the man. Thus, when such qualifications are missing or incomplete, the pastoral candidate should be kept from this office, as he lacks the essential moral integrity before the church and the world.

Charles Bridges, in his classic on the work of the pastor, summarizes my sense of these things well:

> The Scripture justly insists that Ministers should be "holy"—in a peculiar sense men of God—men taught of God; men consecrated to God by a daily surrender of their time and talents to his service; men of singleness and purpose—living in their work; living altogether but for one end. . . . It is evident, however, that this Ministerial standard presupposes a deep tone of experimental and devotional character—habitually exercised in self-denial, prominently marked by love to the Savior, and to the souls of sinners; and practically exhibited in a blameless consistency of conduct.[16]

If we would labor for recovery of truth in our time, and pray for spiritual awakening, both so desperately needed, we must prepare, ordain and preserve, holy ministers. This has never been optional, and it certainly is not optional in a time like the present.

NOTES

1. Janet Clark, "Policies, Principles and Protocol," *Faith Today,* March–April 1994, 22.

2. Tom Carter, Comp.; *Spurgeon at His Best* (Grand Rapids, Mich.: Baker, 1988), 127.

3. Jay E. Smith, "Can Fallen Leaders Be Restored to Leadership?", *Biblotheca Sacra* 151 (October–December 1994): 461.

4. Charles H. Spurgeon, *Lectures to My Students* (Pasadena, Tex.: Pilgrim, 1990 reprint), 23.

5. Thomas D. Lea and Hayne P. Griffin, Jr., *New American Commentary: 1, 2 Timothy and Titus* (Nashville, Tenn.: Broadman/Holman, 1992), 107.

6. Gordon D. Fee, *New International Biblical Commentary:* 1 and 2 Timothy, Titus (Peabody, Mass.: Hendrickson, 1984), 80.

7. Smith, "Can Fallen Leaders Be Restored?" 463.

8. Alfred Plummer, *The Expositor's Bible: The Pastoral Epistles,* W. Robert Nicoll, ed.(London: A. C. Armstrong & Son, 1903), 120–21.

9. Lea and Griffin, *New American Commentary,* 109.

10. Ibid., 109–110.

11. William Hendriksen, *New Testament Commentary* (Grand Rapids, Mich.: Baker, 1957), 121.

12. Lea and Griffin, *New American Commentary,* 114.

13. Ibid., 114.

14. John Newton, *The Works of John Newton,* vol. 5 (Carlisle, Pa.: Banner of Truth, 1988 reprint), 62.

15. Charles Bridges, *The Christian Ministry* (Carlisle, Pa.: Banner of Truth, 1830, reprinted 1976), 24.

16. Ibid., 26–27.

CHAPTER SIX

DISQUALIFIED?

You have a heaven to win yourselves. . . . A holy calling will not save an unholy man.

Richard Baxter

Sexual misconduct entered the life of the church almost from its beginning, two millenia ago. In America, the problem is not new either. From the apparent scandals of the famous minister Henry Ward Beecher down to the massive moral failures of our own time, we have often been forced to address this problem whether we wish to or not. In the midst of a hostile and godless culture the church has always waged battles for moral purity in her leaders. In a pagan environment where tolerance for immorality prevailed, as in the ancient world of the New Testament era, the growing Christian movement naturally faced problems similar to those raised by pastoral adultery in today's permissive society.

The gospel ministry is a calling that demands godly character, as we saw in the previous chapter. Having looked at the prospective pastor and the need for a suitable character, we must now turn our focus on the current pastor and ask: "Is there any ungodly behavior, engaged in by a pastor, that may disqualify him from the pastorate?"

THE ANSWERS FROM IMPROPER DEDUCTION

Most of the articles, interviews, and full length treatments dealing with the issue of disqualification from pastoral ministry approach the subject in terms of potential restoration. The proponents of restoration follow several lines of reasoning in their reply to the above question. As we saw in chapter 2, modern evangelicals tend to respond to the subject of disqualification along three lines: (1) Immediate restoration to ministry (that is, in fewer than twelve months). (2) Ultimate restoration to ministry after an absence of a short duration, perhaps up to 3 years. (3) Spiritual restoration but lifetime disqualification from pastoral office and ministry.

The arguments attached to these three views and the debate that rages tend to increase practical confusion. Pastors debate the issues among themselves, while lay leaders are often traumatized when they actually face the sexual misconduct problem. They simply do not know how to deal with the damage that has been brought to the local church.

SUPPOSE NOW [YOUR PASTOR] HAS SMASHED HIS REPUTATION MORALLY. HIS ETHICAL SOUNDNESS IS DESTROYED. CAN HE BE DISQUALIFIED FROM PASTORAL OFFICE?

The debate between numbers 1 and 2 above, and number 3, which is obviously the more radical response regarding restoration, is often made to hinge on such phrases as "permanent disqualification," "mandatory sentence" and "remaining qualified" or "becoming requalified."

I would like to shift the focus a bit and ask, "Can a man *ever* disqualify himself from pastoral office?" Is there any scenario, any action persisted in, any unethical behavior pattern, or developed lifestyle, that disqualifies a pastor from serving the church as a pastor? Though this may not, at first glance, appear to be a significant shift in emphasis, it is.

Every pastor—your pastor—should be initially qualified through careful examination according to 1 Timothy 3 and Titus 1, as described in the previous chapter. Your pastor is qualified and has served the congregation well. Suppose now he has smashed his reputation morally. His ethical soundness is destroyed. Can he be disqualified from pastoral office? And if disqualification is possible, can a man so ruin his character and reputation that he can never meet the requirements of 1 Timothy 3 and Titus 1?

Answer 1: Forgive and Restore Immediately

The approach taken by those advocating the "immediately forgiven and restored as soon as possible" view is to argue that no matter what the reasons for moral failure a pastor can and should be forgiven and restored to office. As stark as it seems, this view says that to be forgiven is to be qualified.

If this view is true then one would reasonably expect Paul's requirements for office to be simply "forgiven." Period. End of discussion.

With this approach, when examination for ordination takes place, we could well ask: "Have you repented of your sins?" "Have you been forgiven of all unrighteousness?"

Having received an affirmative answer, how can we take the examination of character any further since the man is a brother, loved and forgiven by God?

Answer 2: Forgive and Restore Over Time

With the second approach, the assumption seems to be this: You must repent, and you will be forgiven; but it will take some time to heal the damage in your life. Time, spiritual growth, personal healing, marital counseling and professional therapy, as well as discovery of your newly forgiven status in Christ, all open the door for you to pastor again.[1]

In the case of both of the above responses I submit that there is a great deal of proof-texting on both sides of the argument. Those who wish to argue for remaining in office, or even for return after several years, both wish to appeal to the silence of the text of Scripture regarding the question. They appeal, as well, to very limited views of grace and forgiveness without addressing concerns that go beyond these.

It is true the New Testament nowhere plainly answers our question, in the sense that we frame this question. Nowhere does a text say, "If a pastor commits this particular sin he shall never be a pastor again." Furthermore, as noted previously, no example of a sexually fallen pastor even exists in the accounts of the New Testament. Nowhere do we find statements that plainly tell us that a man must be removed from pastoral office subsequent to moral failure. Of course, it can also be argued, using this same kind of methodology, that the New Testament nowhere sanctions returning a sexually fallen pastor to leadership. Appeals based on such observations, including frequent proof-texting, are often made in a reductionistic manner that never seriously develops concern for New Testament ethical foundations. Conservative Christian thinkers have often reverted to a kind of scholastical moralizing when it comes to addressing difficult ethical matters. We tend to want simple solutions for every moral exigency that arises without having to think through our response. We have not developed a doctrinal/ethical approach that is grounded in the life of Christ and the ethical imperatives of the New Testament in particular. What we have is a kind of conservative "canon law" of opinion that provides ready answers for virtually every moral decision without the need for searching the Scripture in dependence upon the Holy Spirit.

DEVELOPING AN ETHICAL APPROACH

Howard Marshall, a well-known British New Testament scholar, addresses the type of problem I am referring to when he writes:

> The New Testament was not conceived as a textbook (or set of textbooks) of ethics. Its readers are certainly given plenty of instruction on how to live as Christians, but it does not deal systematically with the

issues. The teaching is also given in a variety of modes such as pre-scriptive rules, stories with ethical implications and narratives of behaviour by Christian believers which may or may not be 'approved conduct.'[2]

The tendency among conservative Christians is to treat the New Testament as a book of laws, a kind of neat summation of specific codes for all decisions. We bring our question to the Scriptures, we find the right text which provides a simple answer to our question, then we are free to decide what we shall do in every specific instance. This all-too-common approach pays very little notice to the specific contexts of New Testament passages and reduces important ethical decisions, like ours, to a set of assumed rules.

What is to be observed in the New Testament is often a series of universal principles, given within a cultural and theological framework. These principles must be applied by the guidance of the Holy Spirit to the life of the church in every age. This will require a more careful consideration of the nuances of our particular problems and the significance of numerous important texts, and their ethical weight, that bear upon the church in our culture. This is frequently not accomplished by the endless theoretical debates that often surround the issue of disqualification from pastoral office.

We need to develop an ethical approach to pastoral ministry. What I am appealing for is a more reasoned discussion that looks at restoration to pastoral ministry in the light of broader concerns than forgiveness and the gifts of the fallen pastor being used again.

Richard Longenecker, in addressing the matter of ethics, writes:

> The ethical statements of the New Testament are to be taken with prescriptive and obligatory force, and not just as tactical suggestions which may or may not be heeded by Christians. That is the truth of the position which takes the New Testament as a book of laws for ethical conduct—though to express this truth in the way in which that first position does seriously distorts the true nature of Christian morality. Second, the ethical statements of the New Testament are given not as detailed codes of conduct but as principles or precepts which seek pri-

marily to set a standard for the kind of life pleasing to God, to indicate the direction in which we ought to be moving, and to signal the quality of life our actions ought to be expressing. That is the truth of the position which wants to abstract universal principles from the various ethical statements and actions of the New Testament—though, again, to state this truth in a way which turns theology into philosophy and special revelation into natural law seriously distorts Christian morality.[3]

Longenecker further argues that what we have in the area of New Testament ethics is

. . . a declaration of the gospel and the ethical principles that derive from the gospel, and a description of how that proclamation and its principles were put into practice in various situations during the apostolic period (emphasis his). . . . It will not do to simply ask, Does the New Testament say anything explicit concerning this or that social issue? with the intent being to repeat that answer if it does and to remain silent if it doesn't. Such an approach assumes the record to be a static codification of ethical maxims.[4]

LIKE BELIEVERS IN THE EARLY CHURCH, WE MUST WORK OUT THE IMPLICATIONS OF THE GOSPEL FOR THE SITUATIONS WE ENCOUNTER IN THE CHURCH TODAY. THIS WILL MEAN THAT WE MUST HAVE A BIBLICALLY INFORMED SEXUAL ETHIC THAT CONSIDERS MORE THAN PAT ANSWERS.

These declarations and principles are to be understood as normative for behavior and ethical decision making. We must go beyond merely asking, "How did first-century believers put these principles into action?" We must also ask reverently and prayerfully, "How shall we put these normative principles into action in our age and what are the implications of our actions for the gospel?"

Like believers in the early church, we must work out the implications of the gospel for the situations we encounter in the church today. This will mean that we must have a biblically informed sexual ethic that considers more than pat answers. We must be concerned with questions such as: "What will the implications of our present approach be for the future of the church?" "How will our present approach impact the future of the people directly affected by this man's life?" "What will be the effect of our approach upon the next generation of pastors if we continue to return sexually fallen men, and often quickly, to the pastoral office?" "What do we say about grace and forgiveness when we do not seek to restore a fallen man to office?" We must honestly ask, "What impact does our thinking and practice in this ethical area have upon this generation?"

In the case of the evangelical consensus the answer is quite plain—upon subsequent repentance we must forgive *and* restore, sooner or later. Let's return to the third argument: if a man falls, no matter what the circumstances, under no future scenario can he ever again be a pastor. In this case no consideration of how he fell, where or why, makes any significant difference. That he fell, and that into a heinous sin of incredible rebellion against the Lord of the church, is weighed so seriously that in the end it is predetermined ethically that this person can never be a pastor again. It seems to me, for the same reasons stated, this view wishes to absolutize an ethical decision without further consideration of several important issues. As such, it fails to recognize a biblical ethic by which to evaluate the issues.

Before we consider several key texts that bear upon the issue of disqualification, we need to note that permanent disqualification, based on certain sins committed by an elder/pastor, does have a long tradition, as we will see in the next chapter. For now I am simply trying to answer the question that I think is foundational to our whole consideration: "Does any sin disqualify a pastor?" If a man is disqualified, then we only later can ask, "Can he ever be restored to office?" All I wish to establish for now is whether pastors who fall sexually have disqualified themselves, for at least an extended season, from the pastoral ministry.

A SOBER WARNING

The apostle Paul gives a most sober warning to the Corinthians when he writes:

> Do you not know that those who run in a race all run, but only one receives the prize? Run in such a way that you may win. And everyone who competes in the games exercises self-control in all things. They then do it to receive a perishable wreath, but we an imperishable. Therefore I run in such a way, as not without aim; I box in such a way, as not beating the air; but I buffet my body and make it my slave, lest possibly, after I have preached to others, I myself should be disqualified. (1 Corinthians. 9:24–27)

It appears that the lack of diligent and persevering restraint of the flesh may well land one in the position of disqualification. We must carefully consider what is meant by this word *disqualification*. We must ask several pertinent theological questions of this text. Before we even look at the text, I ask you to ponder a simple fact—a minister of the gospel, not properly restraining his flesh, may very well face catastrophic consequences in his life of service to God. Paul certainly believed that he could be disqualified in some sense.

Disqualification Is Possible

It is a simple fact—the possibility of some type of disqualification does exist! How final and lasting this is, and what the implications are for our present concerns, must be carefully and prayerfully worked out in an ethical framework. In doing this we dare not ignore the warnings of Paul's counsel.

The context of this passage is one in which Paul is addressing the matter of Christian liberty. Verse 23 says it well when Paul writes, "I do all things for the sake of the gospel, that I may become a fellow partaker of it." Paul has been pressing upon his readers the need to use one's freedom in Christ to look after the interests of other brothers and sisters. Now he says, in effect, "Be sure you also look after your own spiritual interests as well." Any minister who wishes to be effective in an ongoing ministry to other brothers and sisters must take care of his own spiritual life; if he does not, his ministry can be put in jeopardy.

His appeal, made to a Gentile audience, is based upon an illustration most likely taken from the Isthmian games, held near Corinth every two years. These games consisted of several events, ranging from discus-throwing to wrestling. Paul's allusion appeals to two of these events, running (v. 24) and boxing (vv. 26–27). He argues in verse 24 that all Christians should run the race—that is, live their lives—ethically and doctrinally, with determination to reach their goal. Hodge says, "In the Christian race there are many victors; but the point of the exhortation is, that all should run as the one victor ran in the Grecian games."[5]

In verse 25 his purpose is to show that all participants must train and thus they must "exercise self-control in all things." The games required rigorous self discipline if an athlete would win. Usually ten months before the games took place a competitor would follow a prescribed diet, abstain from various bodily indulgences, and go through a most difficult routine of physical exercise. Thirty days before the games began each participant would go to the gymnasium every day, attending the exercises that would prepare him for the actual events he would compete in.

Leon Morris comments:

> The strenuous self-denial of the athlete in training for his fleeting reward is a rebuke to all half-hearted, flabby Christian service. Notice that the athlete denies himself many lawful pleasures. The Christian must avoid not only definite sin, but anything that hinders his complete effectiveness.[6]

The race is difficult and the prize is of immense worth. Christian believers run a race of much greater consequence. Surely we can train ourselves to run so that we might win.

Then in verse 26 Paul says that he does not run the Christian race as one who does not know where the finish line is. Nor does he box as one who punches the air, like a shadow-boxer flailing away with no intention of landing a real punch.

The apostle is not suggesting that the body is evil. It is not a thing to be punished through some kind of rigid asceticism that treats it as inherently evil. It has been suggested that the Middle-Age flagellants and similar self-torturers used this very text to justify their excessive and extreme practice.

The answer to this interpretation is quite simple: Paul is not speaking here literally—we should beat our body—but spiritually and figuratively. We must say no even when it costs us deeply, and it will. We must be prepared to deny our flesh continually or we may be led into serious sin with profound consequences.

But what is the reason for this radical call to self-denial?[7] Paul tells the Christian that, like the athlete, he should devote himself to serious self-discipline and persevering effort in order to: (1) receive an "imperishable" wreath; and (2) avoid being "disqualified." What is meant by an "imperishable wreath" here? And what is he potentially "disqualified" from? The answers have an important bearing on the potential restoration of the sexually fallen pastor.

The argument of verse 25 is from the lesser to the greater. If athletes train for a wreath or reward of wild olive or pine wood, then how much greater is the reward which is imperishable and "an inheritance which is imperishable and undefiled and will not fade away, reserved in heaven" (1 Peter 1:4). It is often believed that this term refers to a crown given to some believers who are faithful, but not to all. This idea does not fit the text well. The New Testament writers often use this term to describe things like righteousness, eternal life, and glory (cf. 2 Timothy 4:8; James 1:12; 1 Peter 5:4; Revelation 2:10). Fee is surely correct when he writes: "In this metaphor the Christian's "crown" is not some specific aspect of the goal but the eschatological victory itself. . . . The figure is intended to press upon them that the goal, being eternal in nature, is of such value that it should affect the way they live in the present.[8]

"Disqualified from the Prize"

The second thing Paul labors for in restraining his flesh with all diligence is that he will not be "disqualified" (v. 27).

Paul applies his illustration regarding the games and the requisite discipline needed to win the victor's crown, to himself. He shows that he does not run without focusing intently and purposefully on his goal. He disciplines himself so that he personally will not be "disqualified" (from *adokimos*, meaning rejected, unqualified, or cast off). The allusion here seems clear—the participants must be examined at the end of the contest. "If it was revealed that the winner did not contend according to the rules of the game, he forfeited his crown."[9]

The word for disqualified, or rejected, refers to something/ someone who fails the test and is rejected, or cast off, i.e., "disqualified from the prize." Debates about the nature of this disqualification swirl around the issue of salvation, the security of the believer, and the grace of God. As we will see, though, whatever interpretation you accept, a strong argument is made from the greater moral danger to the lesser one: if a minister can live in a manner that brings "disqualification" in the life to come—whether this is understood as loss of spiritual reward or spiritual salvation—then he can engage in certain immoral behavior that could disqualify him from preaching to others during his earthly life.

Does Paul actually mean that one who is an apostle can fail to obtain the prize? Fee writes:

> Some would say no, but usually because of a prior theological commitment, and not because of what the text actually says. While it is true that in 10:13, after the severe warnings spelled out in vv. 1–12, he once again puts his confidence in God to "keep them," it would be sheer folly to suggest thereby that the warnings are not real. Paul keeps warning and assurance in tension.[10]

On the other side, many commentators side with the historic position of Calvin. They properly oppose any entrance of human contribution to salvation and see this text a bit differently. David Prior writes:

> It is important to avoid the danger of drawing a wrong conclusion from Paul's words here, i.e. that you can end up disqualified (*adokimos*, 27). . . . There is a particularly close word link between 9:27 and 3:13 which makes the meaning of Paul's teaching unambiguous. The

context in 3:11–15 is the way any Christian, but particularly those involved in church-building, will have to face extremely thorough examination about the quality of his work for the Lord. This will be "tested" by fire (*dokimaset*), to a degree which will expose the materials used in building on the foundation, the only foundation which can be laid, Jesus Christ himself. The root word from which both *dokimazei* (3:13) and *adokimos* (9:27) are taken appears in 2 Corinthians 13:5–7, where it occurs five times in a context where the validity of Paul's own apostleship is being queried. A man in Christ cannot lose his salvation, but he can find that his service for Christ has been followed through with his own resources and for his own glory. That is supremely what Paul feared.[11]

IF IT IS POSSIBLE TO BE DISQUALIFIED IN THE FINAL DAY, THEN IT IS POSSIBLE TO BE DISQUALIFIED IN THIS AGE IN TERMS OF ONE'S CHRISTIAN MINISTRY.

Interestingly, Charles Hodge, a Reformed theologian who believed in the security and perseverance of believers, also understood this passage to relate to our eschatological goal—not simply heavenly rewards but our final salvation.

> What an argument and what a reproof is this! The reckless and listless Corinthians thought they could safely indulge themselves to the very verge of sin, while this devoted apostle considered himself as engaged in a life-struggle for his salvation. This same apostle, however, who evidently acted on the principle that the righteous scarcely are saved, and that the kingdom of heaven suffereth violence, at other times breaks out in the most joyful assurance of salvation, and says that he was persuaded that nothing in heaven, earth or hell could ever separate him from the love of God (Rom. 8:38,39). The one state of mind is the necessary condition of the other. It is only those who are conscious of this constant and deadly struggle with sin, to whom this assurance is given. In the very same breath Paul says, "O wretched man that I am;" and, "Thanks be to God who giveth us the victory (Rom. 7:24, 35). It is the indolent and self-indulgent Christian who is always in doubt.[12]

Whatever your position, do not lose sight that the apostle Paul is issuing a very serious warning. The view of many Protestant commentators is like that of Fee, Godet and Hodge. Others, like Prior, argue that "disqualification" refers to the loss of reward for service in the final day. Both have in view the eschatological implications of being "rejected after testing."[13] Colin Brown says the idea is "that which has not stood the test, that which has been shown to be a sham and has therefore been rejected" is disqualified.[14]

Paul does not say here that he might be disqualified from his present apostleship, nor does he state what sins in particular might actually cause this eschatological disqualification. For this reason many have argued that this passage has nothing to do with the question of ministerial office and potential disqualification in the *present* age. One commonly advanced position says, "Nothing in the context which goes before lends itself to the idea that the person is disqualified from ever competing in the event (ministry)."

Strictly speaking that is true, but it fails to grasp the larger consequences of the ethical concerns in the context. Paul is already in the race. That is certain. The real question is how will he continue, and in particular, how will he finish.

If Paul is concerned to "buffet his body" in order that he not be ultimately disqualified in the day of judgment, then it logically stands to reason that he could be disqualified by scandalous behavior that does not "buffet his body" regarding his present ministry. Present ministry does have significant bearing on the final judgment, or this passage means nothing at all.[15]

As Christians, we know that the Scriptures argue that if we made a true profession of faith, we will demonstrate that faith in good works. (See particularly James 1:21–25; 12:14–20; and 1 John 2:19–20.) Without such works, and if evil deeds and ongoing sinful behavior characterize our lives, the strong possibility exists that we never had true saving faith to begin with. In the final day we may find ourselves disqualified.

I appeal from the greater moral danger—living in a manner that brings "disqualification" in the life to come—to the lesser danger—namely, that certain immoral behavior could disqualify one from preaching to others in this age. If it is possible to be disqualified in the final day, and we have seen that it is, then it is possible to be "disqualified" in this age in terms of one's Christian ministry.

"But," you may wish to argue, "one has been examined and found qualified to hold pastoral ministry in this age, according to criteria of 1 Timothy 3:2 and following. Even if he be disqualified in the age to come, how can a pastor cease to be qualified in this life as well?" Given the New Testament's concern for purity in faith and practice among those who serve as overseers of the church of God, this deduction is patently plain. The qualifications required for ministry imply the potential of subsequent disqualification based on the principles seen in 1 Corinthians 9:24–27.

THE THREAT OF APOSTASY
A Real Danger

Furthermore, the danger of spiritual apostasy is real. The warnings of Scripture to "be all the more diligent to make certain about His calling and choosing you" (2 Peter 1:10) and the counsel of Paul to "continue in the faith, firmly established and steadfast, and not moved away from the hope of the gospel that you have heard" (Colossians 1:23) are admonitions that support the concerns 1 Corinthians 9 sets before us. The New Testament contains actual illustrations of men who were disqualified from ministry by virtue of some kind of failure, either doctrinal or ethical. (See, for instance, 1 Timothy 1:20 and 2 Timothy 2:17.) Who can doubt that Judas, who had the power to preach and perform powerful apostolic signs, disqualified himself both temporally and eternally. His profession, which appeared sound to all who knew him outwardly, proved to be without foundation. He was an apostate, one who seemed to follow Christ but never believed in Him as the Savior of the world.

It is frightening to realize that few evangelical ministers today preach regarding these dangers, and even fewer consider the danger to themselves of final apostasy—the discovery that they never believed, even though their participation in grievous sins suggested they may not have truly believed. Our Lord's awful warning stands clear:

Not everyone who says to Me, "Lord, Lord," will enter the kingdom of heaven, but he who does the will of My Father who is in heaven. Many will say to Me on that day, "Lord, did we not prophesy in Your name, and in Your name cast out demons, and in Your name perform many miracles?" And then I will declare unto them, "I never knew you: Depart from Me, you who practice lawlessness." (Matthew 7:21–23)

It is rare to hear these words taken with profound seriousness in our day. We have reason, both in this text and in the ethical and doctrinal confusion of our own time, to think that the "many" of our Lord's warning is descriptive of some ministries in this age.

MEN WHO FALL SEXUALLY WHILE IN THE PASTORAL MINISTRY GENERALLY SHOULD REMOVE THEMSELVES IMMEDIATELY, IF FOR NO OTHER REASON THAN TO MAKE SURE THAT THEY PROTECT THEMSELVES FROM FURTHER FAILURE THAT OFTEN RECURS IF THEY REMAIN IN OFFICE.

The danger of apostasy is so serious that I am convinced that men who fall sexually while in the pastoral ministry generally should remove themselves immediately, if for no other reason than to make sure that they protect themselves from further failure that often recurs if they remain in office. A greater fall often recurs when fallen pastors do not take more seriously the implications of their lapse.

In general, men who fall sexually have followed a pattern of deception, misinformation, and outright lying for months, if not years. Should they confess their sin, and then be restored to pastoral labor prematurely, which I have argued is the common approach in our time, they run another risk—that of experiencing too quick a healing that may well result in destruction later. It is beneficial to "mourn" if we would be genuinely "comforted" (Matthew 5:4).

If you are a minister who is showing a wrong pattern of living—a lifestyle that dismisses or tolerates sin—you should excuse yourself from public ministry, both to save your flock from a poor model and to devote yourself to determining your relationship with the Savior. A church committee should enforce such a position for the spirtual welfare of the pastor—and their church.

A Quick Response

The personal and spiritual dangers of prompt restoration with such sin are so severe that ministers who recognize this historic biblical teaching usually take themselves out of the pastoral ministry immediately. Quite simply, they do not trust themselves, and they can't even begin to consider how they could ever trust themselves again, especially with spiritual leadership in the church. When we consider how sexual sin permeates the entire human personality (see 1 Corinthians 6:18–20) we need to weigh this matter far more soberly than we do. All sin is deceitful, but sexual sin seems particularly able to deceive and to harden the human heart of those caught in its follies. It captures those who partake of it, destroying them in ways that have lifetime effects, and it brings spiritual chaos to the lives of all who are directly associated with them. Marital infidelity is truly a fire of destruction that touches the soul deeply.

It is interesting that John Calvin, commenting upon this text, adds these words of pastoral counsel:

> My life [as a minister] ought to be a kind of rule to others. Accordingly, I strive to conduct myself in such a manner, that my character and conduct may not be inconsistent with my doctrine, and that thus I may not be inconsistent with my doctrine, and that thus I may not, with great disgrace to myself, and a grievous occasion of offense to my brethren, neglect those things which I require from others.[16]

If I, as a pastor, am to require others to live godly lives consistent with the gospel I proclaim then I must be more than a simple "communicator" of Christian philosophy. The gospel must become, as with Paul, "my gospel." I must not simply teach it. I must plainly live it out in such a way that I will not face disqualification, either in the future judgment, or in the present ministry of the church.

NOTES

1. For an amplification of this position, see chapters 9 and 12 of Tim LaHaye, *If Ministers Fall, Can They Be Restored?* (Grand Rapids, Mich.: Zondervan, 1990). LaHaye gives the official procedure of the Assemblies of God as one example of the process officially followed. Also, in "How Pure Must a Pastor Be?" *Leadership,* Spring 1988, 12–20, several pastors indicate the procedure followed by their denominations. Most evangelical denominations seem only now to be formulating position papers and practice on this problem, while mainline denominations, in general, addressed it several years ago. I have found that outside the United States many historic denominations already have position papers and in general make it quite difficult for a person to return to pastoral office if they have fallen into sexual immorality. Time periods for absence from office are generally encouraged for one to three years.

2. I. Howard Marshall, "New Occasions Teach New Duties? The Use of the New Testament in Christian Ethics," *The Expository Times,* 105 (February 1994): 132.

3. Richard N. Longenecker, *New Testament Social Ethics for Today* (Grand Rapids, Mich.: Eerdmans, 1984), 14–15.

4. Ibid., 26–27.

5. Charles Hodge, *Commentary on the First Epistle to the Corinthians* (Grand Rapids, Mich.: Eerdmans, 1969 reprint), 167.

6. Leon Morris, *The First Epistle of Paul to the Corinthians* (Grand Rapids, Michigan: Eerdmans, 1958), 139.

7. The radical call to denying oneself begins with Jesus' teaching in Matthew 5:29-30, given in a setting that plainly addresses the matter of sexual lust and the ensuing temptation that follows. The Lord says that it is better to tear out and throw away your eye or cut off your hand "than for your whole body to go into hell" (Matthew 5:29–30). His message is figurative, as He tells us that to follow him away from the wide road that leads to hell will require radical surgery carried out in the power of the Spirit. This is a necessary part of sanctification. Because salvation is the present possession of all who truly trust in Him alone does not make it irrelevant that we still must "work out our salvation with fear and trembling" (Philippians 2:12). (We do not work "for" our salvation, but we do "work out" in progressive, definitive sanctification what the Spirit of God has worked in us through regenerating grace.)

8. Gordon Fee, *The First Epistle to the Corinthians* (Grand Rapids, Mich.: Eerdmans, 1987), 437.

9. Curtis Vaughan and Thomas D. Lea, *Bible Study Commentary: 1 Corinthians* (Grand Rapids, Mich.: Zondervan, 1983), 98.

10. Fee, *The First Epistle,* 440.

11. David Prior, *The Message of 1 Corinthians,* (Downers Grove, Ill.: InterVarsity , 1985), 163–64.

12. Hodge, Commentary, 169.

13. G. Abbott Smith, *Manual Greek Lexicon of the New Testament* (New York: Charles Scribner's Sons, 1922), 10.

14. Colin Brown, ed., *The New International Dictionary of New Testament Theology* (Exeter, England: Paternoster, 1978), 808.

15. Jay E. Smith, "Can Fallen Leaders Be Restored to Leadership?", *Bibliotheca Sacra* 151 (October–December 1994): 466–67. Smith argues that the obvious reference here is eschatological, with which I am in full agreement. He proceeds to say that the text therefore has no bearing on the issue of disqualification from preaching, or leadership, in the present age, a conclusion I do not think is warranted, as I show.

16. John Calvin, *Commentary on the Epistles of Paul the Apostle to the Corinthians* (Grand Rapids, Mich.: Baker, 1979 reprint), 311.

CHAPTER SEVEN

AND NOW
A WORD
FROM THE PAST

To test the present you must appeal to history.

Winston Churchill

*H*istorian Herbert Butterfield wrote, "What history does is to uncover man's universal sinfulness." History also uncovers the beauty of God's grace in man's predicament and God's faithfulness in advancing His own kingdom. In history we see God displaying mercy to His people even when they have fallen far away from Him. When reformation has taken place and the Scriptures have been recovered, in any era, new light dawns in believing hearts, and change is inevitable as the Spirit is poured out with fresh power.

However, many have assumed that history and tradition should have no bearing on present faith and practice. "After all, they argue, "evangelicalism has a single source of authority, namely the sacred Scriptures. Since the Reformation, every doctrine the Protestant church embraces must be revealed by Scripture." This view, held by most of the Church Fathers as well, is at the heart of what is meant by *sola scriptura,* "the Scriptures alone." Nonetheless, until this century, Protestant evangelicalism has never believed that church tradition is irrelevant or useless.

In Protestant evangelicalism, history and tradition have held a very high subsidiary role to the exposition of Scripture. They are vital aids, collections of the Spirit's wisdom given to the church militant, but never rival sources of revelation.

What does this mean for the question at hand? Simply that the church's historic efforts at understanding this matter of sexually fallen pastors should inform how we think about the present question. We must do serious and careful exegesis of the text before we respond to this problem. We must also develop a better ethical approach that considers the life of the entire congregation and its ministry. Furthermore, we must do this work with the assistance of the church's collective insight from centuries of faith and practice. We must not, pridefully, treat the present problem as if we are the first Christians to ever deal thoughtfully with the issue of sexual misconduct in pastoral ministry.

Our age is surely not the first one to face moral lapses in the manse. Records from the early church reveal that this problem brought down the ministry of overseers in the church from the very beginning. And it has visited its devastation upon the flock in every age since. Some periods of time have been notoriously problematic, others less so, but in days of darkness as well as in days of revival, this problem has been with us. All of this means that we are not living in an era all that different, in one sense, from other days in the past. What may be different is the knowledge that we have of this problem, as well as the way in which we presently tolerate it.

In this chapter we will consider historical dealings with moral failure in the pastoral ministry, taken from three eras of church history—the early church, the Protestant Reformers and the Reformation, and from early American history. These are certainly not the only eras that could be studied, but they are the three in which we get closest to a deep concern for biblical fidelity and personal holiness. They are also the three eras that provide the most resource for our observation.

The questions we ask are: How did the church deal with this vexing problem of sexually fallen pastors, and were such men disqualified from holding office? Were they ever encouraged toward restoration to office? What, in general, was the church's attitude toward adultery in a pastor who had been "set apart" as an overseer?

THE EARLY CHURCH

Notably the early church held to complete disqualification from pastoral ministry when an elder had sinned sexually. The evidence for this observation is unambiguous. We will consider only some of the evidence. We shall seek to put it into a context that speaks to our present time.

ONE OF THE SINS OFTEN ASSOCIATED WITH FALSE TEACHERS WAS SEXUAL IMMORALITY. IT WAS, FOR THE APOSTLE PETER, A KIND OF DISTINGUISHING CHARACTERISTIC OF THE FALSE TEACHER.

We must remember that the early church wrestled with major doctrinal battles that touched the very essence of the burgeoning Christian faith and practice. There was no time for triviality or unimportant discussion. Every decision made was a matter of life and death. Pastors and everyday members were being put to death at regular intervals as powerful emperors came and went. The culture threatened to destroy the faith via the sword. Errorists from within the church threatened to destroy it via heresy. Sexual immorality was a swamp of pollution in the Roman world. It had to be avoided at every turn.

A religion like Christianity, which treated the body as holy and good yet at the same time taught that the body was to be kept free from sexual relations outside the estate of marriage, was most rare in the ancient world. The mystery religions were ardent rivals and openly accommodated the sexually explicit practice of the time. Christianity, in its primary texts and early development, could tolerate no moral aberrations or it would not survive in such a climate.

The New Testament church experienced severe troubles with false teachers. One of the sins often associated with false teachers was sexual immorality. It was, for the apostle Peter, a kind of distinguishing characteristic of the false teacher, many of whom would "follow their sensuality, and because of them the way of truth [would] be maligned." (See 2 Peter 2:1–2.) Peter later described these troublers of the church as:

> springs without water, and mists driven by a storm, for whom black darkness has been reserved. For speaking out arrogant words of vanity they entice by fleshly desires, by sensuality, those who barely escape from the ones who live in error, promising them freedom while they themselves are slaves of corruption; for by what a man is overcome, by this he is enslaved (2 Peter 2:17–19).

Throughout 2 Peter 2 the apostle connected sensuality, or "immoral ways" and "dissolute conduct" (Weymouth), with the work of false teaching. Teaching and conduct plainly go together. What these first-century false teachers taught they also practiced. In verse 7 Peter connected their behavior to Sodom and Gomorrah, and in verse 18 he says of these same false teachers that "while they pour out their frivolous and arrogant talk, they use sensual pleasures—various kinds of immorality—as a trap for men who are just escaping from those who live in error" (Weymouth). They are, further, "slaves of corruption" who have been "overcome" by sensual activity. True Christianity must combine sound doctrine with sound living. These men have already been described as being men who have "eyes full of adultery, eyes such as cannot cease from sin" (v. 14).

There is very plainly a relationship that exists between false teaching and loose living sexually. D. Martyn Lloyd-Jones saw this connection when he wrote:

> From the standpoint of mere mechanics it is very difficult at times to see which of the two comes first. False teaching always leads to false living; yes, but false living always tends to produce false teaching. . . . How is all of this to be avoided? Here Peter gives us very detailed instructions. The thing we have to do is realize the character of false teaching. We must examine it, we must sift it, and investigate it, and

this is the thing that so many find difficult. It is not an easy thing for a man to be different from others. . . . We may have to be like Lot in Sodom. We may have to stand as some of those first Christians had to stand. We may have to stand as some of the Protestant Fathers had to stand; we may even have the church condemning us. No, it is not easy, and yet it is the very thing which we are exhorted to do. We must not believe everything we hear, we must examine it by the Word of God.[1]

It is not surprising, then, that the apostle Paul sets forth requirements for the office of pastor (cf. 1 Timothy 3:2–7) that particularly stress moral qualifications in the area of sexual practice. When he writes to the believers in Thessalonica, he gives the church pointed instruction regarding their sexual conduct. His is not the modern counsel that tends to treat sexual misconduct as one of many sins. Instead he declares:

For you know what commandments we gave you by the authority of the Lord Jesus. For this is the will of God, your sanctification; that is, that you abstain from sexual immorality; that each of you know how to possess his own vessel in sanctification and honor, not in lustful passion, like the Gentiles who do not know God, and that no man transgress and defraud his brother in the matter because the Lord is the avenger in all these things, just as we also told you before and solemnly warned you. For God has not called us for the purpose of impurity, but in sanctification (1 Thessalonians 4: 2–7).

In his impressive study *The History of the Christian Church*, noted church scholar J. J. Foakes Jackson wrote, "Idolatry and the grosser sins of impurity were often considered as unpardonable in this world."[2] Idolatry, or false teaching and false worship, are almost always associated with sexual impurity. This was true in the Old Testament, and if anything, it is more plainly true in the New Testament. As I studied the New Testament on this matter again recently the connection became obvious, and I am almost overwhelmed by the consistently severe way the apostles view sexual impurity. It is not that other sins could not and did not destroy a person, a ministry, or a church, but when sexual misconduct was present the darkness was great and the judgment of the Lord most obvious!

Carl Volz, a contemporary Lutheran historian, has done extensive research on the early church and its approach to ethics, especially pastoral ethics. After citing Peter's counsel that God requires holiness in those who follow Him (1 Peter 1:15), Volz writes, "The specific ramifications of this demanding ethic were to be determined by each believer, following general guidelines of the Ten Commandments. . . . " Because this general pattern needed to be worked out in terms of a culture that threatened the church with extermination on the one hand and impurity on the other, Volz notes that "By the second century this elastic but demanding view of Christian behavior had become more narrow and systematic to the point of rigidity and legalism. A considerable amount of pastoral time and energy was devoted to maintaining the discipline of holiness within the congregation."[3]

Justin's description of early church response to sexual sin is typical. He says: "We who formerly delighted in fornication now embrace purity alone; we who formerly used magic arts now dedicate ourselves to the good and unbegotten God; we who loved the path to wealth and possession above all, now bring what we have into the common stock, and give to any in need."[4]

Roman entertainment was to be avoided in general. The arena, the ancient circus, and especially the vile theater, were shunned by Christians in good fellowship with the church. Women were specifically taught to dress modestly; men were not allowed certain positions because of their association with evil, including makers of idols, charioteers, actors and actresses, military commanders and civil magistrates (due to pagan oaths they had to swear in daily life). Volz then adds:

> The one area that appears to receive the most attention in the early attempts to regulate the Christian life is that of sexual ethics. Early councils appear to contain more decrees on this subject than any other, unless perhaps there may be more regulating the life of the clergy. It may be this is due to an inordinate preoccupation with sex in the minds of puritanical rigorists, but it may also be caused by the fact that Christianity was born within a Roman society in which family stability and moral discipline had given way to flagrant decadence.[5]

A Roman orator, Quintillian, described the conditions of the culture of that time. He spoke of parents corrupting their children through teaching them vices before they could even know that they were vices. Seneca, a famous Roman philosopher during the time of Christ, said, "No woman need blush about breaking her marriage, since most prominent ladies have learned to reckon the years by the names of their husbands."[6] Volz concludes, after a survey of the sexual evil prevalent in the time of the apostles and early church fathers, by saying:

> There can be little wonder that Christian sexual standards appeared to be radical, given this environment. Monogamy was the Christian rule, and infidelity was a grave offense both for husband and wife, just as fornication by a single person was cause for excommunication and severe penance. Divorce was forbidden, and even infidelity was not an automatic cause for separation of spouses.[7]

In the early church a debate raged for several centuries regarding the efficacy of the sacraments when they were administered by an immoral clergyman. The question usually debated was this: Are the sacraments, particularly baptism, acceptable if the person who administered them was immoral, or had become immoral since? (It must be understood that I am not here discussing the question of efficacy and the theology related to this.) This problem truly troubled the church and those affected by it. The discipline of the early church, as seen above, was both firm, immediate, even severe. This was especially so when it came to sexual sin.

A historian, writing in the last century about the works of Tertullian, a famous church father, says that the question of what to do with an adulterous pastor did not surface in his own study. He speculated that the reason for this was that "An openly vicious minister would then have been immediately degraded, and cut off from the communion of the Church. Standing, therefore, on the footing of a heathen, he would have been deemed incapable of administering any of the rites of the Church."[8]

Volz plainly states that the church barred immoral pastors from public ministry "through moral lapse, heresy, or incompetence . . ." He notes, further, that whatever had been conferred in ordination did not protect presbyters from such removal and disqualification should they so fail their Lord and His church.[9]

BASIL, A BISHOP OF THE FIFTH CENTURY, DECREED THAT IMMORAL DEACONS HAD FORFEITED THEIR OFFICE. . . . TERTULLIAN FORBADE THE RESTORATION OF FALLEN PASTORS TO OFFICE.

Among early church men, the words of Hippolytus, Basil, and Tertullian are instructive. Hippolytus, a presbyter in the third-century church of Rome, decried the pastors of his day who lived shamelessly. Yet there were bishops who would not even remove the sinning individuals from ministry. He reported that some believed that a bishop could not lose his office, no matter how great his sin was. He labored and agonized over this desiring a more pure and faithful ministry in his time.[10]

Basil, a bishop of the fifth century, decreed that immoral deacons had forfeited their office as well, but that they should be restored to the fellowship of the church if repentant.[11] Tertullian forbade the restoration of fallen pastors to office. He warned those who advocated a return to church fellowship, "Whatever authority, whatever reason, restores ecclesiastical peace to the adulterer and the fornicator, the same will be bound to come to the aid of the murderer and the idolater in their repentance." Tertullian's words make clear that the church in its early days was anything but tolerant of morally lapsed members, especially if they were pastors. Discipline was perceived as strongly needed precisely because the Scriptures taught it, and the surrounding culture would crush the church without it.[12]

The second-century *Didache*, or *The Teaching of the Apos-tles*, insisted that the pastor who has been ordained and then afterward disobeyed God's Word should be disqualified because "he has lied." In this instance we see that sexual misconduct was such an egregious breach of the third commandment and a violation of the pastor's vows of loyalty and purity before Christ and the church, that his pastoral ministry was finished.[13]

The Council of Elvira, held in Spain in the fourth century after a period of intense persecution, represents the kind of thinking we see in the early church regarding pastoral sexual sin. This council, attended by nineteen bishops and a number of presbyters (by this time the offices had changed from the simple New Testament usage), faced the problems created by rapid conversion growth that was followed by a decline of spiritual fervor. The problem they specifically addressed was this: What degree of compromise can the church tolerate with pagan society? Eighty-one canons were issued by the council, many of them addressing marriage, adultery, and celibacy among the pastoral leaders of the churches. One canon said, "Should bishops, presbyters, or deacons, once installed in office, be discovered to be adulterers, it is resolved, both because of the offense and because of the impious crime, that they not be allowed into communion even at death."[14]

The early church plainly disqualified from membership any who were sexually immoral. Further, those who had fallen and had been restored to the church, which happened only occasionally, were not ever suitable for ordination to the pastoral office. Those men who, having been placed in pastoral office, were sexually immoral were immediately discharged from their position of leadership and placed under the most rigorous and severe discipline of the church. It seems that none of those who had fallen while pastors would ever be restored to that office again.

THE REFORMATION ERA

The Protestant Reformation, begun in Germany in 1517 when Martin Luther took a decisive public stand against abusive and unethical church practices, was what historian Robert Linder has called "a combination of the confluence of events with a man of dynamic personality, considerable talent, and deep religious concerns."[15] But it was much more, at least eventually it was. It was a time of grand recovery, when the gospel of grace was restored to the faith of the church. And it was perhaps the greatest and most widespread awakening of the Holy Spirit since Pentecost.

What motivated this movement? At its core was a desire to return the church to the purity of faith and practice that was based upon the Scriptures of the Old and New Testaments alone, thus the frequently used Latin phrase, *sola Scriptura*. The church had developed the use of tradition to the degree that centuries of false scholastic debate and fatally flawed practice had shut out the glories of the gospel itself. When the light shined into the hearts of believing people once again, the recovery that followed had vast implications for decades to follow.

During these debates, and as a result of the Protestant concern for a faithful and pure leadership in the church, much concern was given again to the ministry of the pastor, first raised by John Wycliffe a century before Luther. The results of this recovery are important for our consideration.

Huldrych Zwingli, one of the earliest Reformers and a man who had been immoral before his conversion, was believed to have been involved in a council in Zurich that oversaw the marital relations of the local community. The charge of infidelity brought severe penalties to the guilty, which included "the loss of all offices as well as excommunication." This would have clearly meant secular office, and reason would dictate that church office was possibly in view because of the church-state position held by Zwingli.[16]

Luther, the German monk who was used to ignite the fires of this scriptural recovery, was profoundly concerned about the ministry of the gospel in the local church. Commenting upon 1 Timothy, he wrote,

Before God no one is above reproach, but before men the bishop is to be so, that he may not be a fornicator, an adulterer, a greedy man, a foul-mouthed person, a drunkard, a gambler, a slanderer. If he is falsely accused, no harm; he is still above reproach; no law can accuse him before men. Samuel and Moses are good examples. Samuel said, "If I have defrauded anyone, etc." (cf. 1 Sam. 12:3). There he showed how innocent he was, as far as men were concerned. Moses spoke this way before Korah (cf. Num. 16:15). To live this way, that you do not harm your neighbor by theft or adultery, means that no man can accuse you of anything or say: "You have stolen from me; you have raped my wife." [17]

Roman Catholicism had so stressed celibacy, and the attendant asceticism that had developed over the centuries, that marriage had come to be seen as an inferior estate. Priests were not allowed to marry, ostensibly because they were married to Christ in service to His church. Luther and those who followed him developed an entirely different view. Returning to the Scriptures, they discovered a high view of husbands and wives and honored marriage as an institution of great profit for all, including pastors.

IN ALL THIS WE DISCOVER, AGAIN, THAT SEXUAL SIN WAS SIMPLY NOT TREATED AS SOME KIND OF MINOR FAILURE ON THE LEVEL OF MOST OTHER CHRISTIAN SINS. THE LUTHERAN REFORM MOVEMENT RESTORED MARRIAGE TO A HIGH LEVEL . . . BUT CLEARLY LIMIT[ED] SEXUAL UNION TO ONE'S SPOUSE.

The Roman Catholic church denied divorce on all grounds, even where adultery was clearly present, preferring to interpret Matthew 5:31–32 and 19:3–9 as allowing no exceptions. Returning to the study of Scripture itself, via careful grammatical and historical principles of interpretation, the Protestant church believed sexual infidelity, by one partner in a lawful marriage, could end the marriage with God's complete approval. Indeed, some went so far as to say sexual adultery did, *ipso facto,* end the marriage, and if the non-guilty partner wished to restore the marriage with the sinning guilty partner a new marriage would be necessary, the first having been destroyed by the sexual sin. This view, held, for example, by Johannes Bugenhagen, one of the most prominent Lutheran catechists of the era, was intended to treat adultery very seriously.

Bugenhagen referred to sexual sin as a man committing "the most shameful act of betrayal." Says Ozment, "Bugenhagen maintained, a husband was no more a husband, nor a wife a wife, than a virgin was a virgin after fornication; something irretrievable left a marriage the moment one of the partners became unfaithful."[18]

In all of this we discover, again, that sexual sin was simply not treated as some kind of minor failure on the level of most other Christian sins. The Lutheran Reform movement restored marriage to a high level, treating sexual relationships as both desirable and good, but clearly limiting sexual union to one's spouse.

It is not surprising, therefore, to find that when we do discover scant references here and there to pastors who are adulterous, the picture is one which is stated in terms of a complete "betrayal" of pastoral position and call. One searches in vain for any kind of practice that would support adulterous pastors returning to office when their sin had plainly devastated their public ministry. Luther's words on the pastoral office offer a number of reasons why a man could, in effect, disqualify himself. One must assume, given the way Luther approaches sins like avarice and idolatry, that this sin was inferred, if not plainly stated in his writing on this subject.

When we come to John Calvin, and the ministry he exercised in Geneva, the evidence for such a conclusion is much plainer. In "The Register of the Company of Pastors," a collection of documents kept between 1541 and 1564, we read,

> In order to obviate all scandals of conduct it will be needful to have
> a form of discipline for ministers . . . to which all are to submit them-

selves. This will help to ensure that the minister is treated with respect and the Word of God is not brought into dishonor and scorn by the evil fame of ministers. Moreover, as discipline will be imposed on him who merits it, so also there will be need to suppress slanders and false reports that may justly be uttered against those who are innocent.

It must be noted that there are crimes which are altogether intolerable in a minister [e.g. heresy, schism, open blasphemy, treachery, perjury, drunkenness, assault punishable by laws, usury, offenses bearing civil infamy and fornication, etc.] and faults which may be endured [e.g. buffoonery, negligence in study of the scripture, rashness, dissolute language, deceitfulness, defamation, evil scheming, uncontrolled anger, etc.] provided a fraternal admonition is offered.[19]

Commenting on why the above list is given for the discipline of Geneva's Protestant Reformed ministers, Calvin added:

With regard to offenses which ought under no circumstances to be tolerated, if they are civil offenses, that is to say, those which are punishable by the law, and any minister is guilty of them, the Seigneury [body of elders] shall take the matter in hand and, over and above the ordinary punishment customarily imposed on others, shall punish him by deposing him from his office.[20]

It is interesting that Calvin saw this as being so important for the well-being of the church that he appointed a time (which occurred every three months) and a place where the elders were to "give special attention to see whether there is anything open to criticism among themselves, so that, as is right, it may be remedied."[21]

CALVIN CONCLUDED [THAT] . . . MINISTERIAL ADULTERY CUT ONE OFF FROM THE OFFICE OF PASTOR AND THE BENEFITS OF THE CHURCH.

In his helpful commentary on the pastoral letters Calvin deals with the requirement for the pastor to be "above reproach" or "blameless." He writes that the term is "properly an antagonistic term, signifying, 'one who gives his adversary no hold upon him;' but it is often (as here) applied metaphorically

to one who gives others no cause justly to accuse him." By all
of this Calvin means that the church must examine the man's
life carefully lest any "remarkable vice" be chargeable against
him which would hinder his future usefulness.[22]

Calvin, like Luther a preacher who engaged almost daily in
this public ministry, preached a series of sermons on the pastoral letters. He rebuked the Roman Catholic Church for its
harsh doctrine that marriage was forbidden to ministers and
said, regarding pastors, that "this is the holiness that God re-
quireth in his servants, and in them whom he hath placed to
preach his Word, to wit, that they keep themselves chaste with
their wives, and live like good husbands."

Clearly Calvin was concerned about the moral standing of
the minister after he had entered the office of pastor. In the
same sermon he added, "They that [who] are appointed ministers of the Word of God must not be intemperate, and given to
lewdness." If they are, Calvin concluded, then the lay people
will become involved in tolerating wickedness which "must be
cut off in them that are church ministers." Simply put, ministerial adultery cut one off from the office of pastor and the
benefits of the church. Discipline, as we saw above, was taken
very seriously and enforced upon sexually fallen pastors with
earnest fidelity to the Word of God.[23]

In conclusion, we can say the Reformers sought to return
to the New Testament's concern for an evident and consistent
moral purity in the lives of those who were pastors. After some
centuries of moral laxity in the church, they attacked this impurity in their reforming efforts and set up procedures for dealing with sexually fallen ministers that would remove such from
office upon the confession of such sin. If such sin were not
admitted but a conviction came through a proper church procedure, which involved fellow elders examining and deciding
the evidence, the minister was immediately removed.

THE NEW ENGLAND PURITAN PERSPECTIVE

Much ignorance exists about the ministry and influence of
Puritan Christianity. At one time the mere mention of the

word "puritan" meant dour at best and prudish at worst. In recent years our understanding of the historic Puritans has changed significantly due to some excellent and accurate treatments of these godly Christians. When it comes to concern for moral purity and proper order in the church, we can learn much from both the English Puritans and those who came to settle New England.

The churches of New England established clear models for discipline, which addressed the subject of pastoral disqualification through moral breakdown. For instance, Chapter 8, Article 7 of "The Cambridge Platform of Church Discipline" reads, "If the church have power to choose their officers and pastors, then in case of manifest unworthiness and delinquency, they have power to depose them."[24] Though the sin of sexual immorality is not plainly stated, we cannot doubt that this sin would have been included, based on the fact that other literature speaks plainly to this matter and Calvin's Geneva was still the major influence upon their thought.

> ONE PURITAN PREACHER BLUNTLY
> DECLARED, "IF HIS LIFE CONTRADICTS HIS
> PREACHING, HE HAD BETTER LAY DOWN HIS
> BIBLE AND LEAVE THE SACRED DESK."

The consistent view and practice of these early Puritans are revealed most plainly in ordination sermons, which allowed them to address concerns about pastoral matters publicly. Cotton Mather observed that "To embrace a man who is not of the best morals merely because he agrees with us" is in fact a serious compromise of proper thinking about Christian unity.[25]

Ordination sermons reveal a connection between disqualification in the final day (that is, eschatologically) and disqualification in the present day because of sexual sin. An example is found in the ordination sermon of a Samuel Cooper who said, "While we are justly severe to gross and scandalous sins, which are peculiarly detestable in the ministers of religion, we shall make all fair allowances for those misapprehensions and small imperfections of our brethren, which are consistent with integrity."[26]

Cooper's statement echoes the earlier warning by Calvin. Sins that do not destroy the character and integrity of the pastor must be dealt with and corrected so that the man might experience fruitfulness in his life and labors. The problem with adultery is that it is in the category of severely punishable sins, and it will erode the integrity of the man and his future ministry should he fall into it as a minister of the gospel.[27]

John Callender certainly did not share the modern idea that a pastor has the right to remain in office when he sins sexually. He preached, "They who disgrace their office should be put out of it."[28] Another Puritan preacher bluntly and openly declared, "If his life contradicts his preaching, he had better lay down his Bible and leave the sacred desk."[29]

Cotton and Increase Mather wrote an entire volume on the danger of flocks being devastated by pastors who were not true shepherds of the flock of Christ. One of the examples they cite is that already noted in 2 Peter 2 and elsewhere. False teachers often divide sheep and destroy the flock of Christ via adulterous behavior with members of the church.[30]

During the revivals of the eighteenth and nineteenth centuries, false and manipulative ministers used the occasion of deep emotion to take advantage of women under their pastoral care. Concern about such behavior can be seen in some of the accounts of the famous Cane Ridge revivals on the Kentucky frontier in the early days of the nineteenth century. It seems that in the American colonies, especially after the young nation was formed in 1787, the further the Christian religion got away from careful doctrinal preaching the more likely it was to play directly on the emotions. This often opened the door all the more to the kind of religious practice that involved men in sexual relationships with women in their congregations. The results of this development have come with full force in our generation.

CONCLUSION

We have seen that the Church Fathers were concerned with sexual sin against the background of an extremely decadent culture that stood in sharp contrast to the biblical ideals of purity and sexual fidelity in marriage. Some saw marriage as the second best choice, while others even drifted into asceticism and legalism. What emerges plainly is this: They would tolerate no deviation from moral purity and certainly would not allow a pastor to continue in office who had fallen sexually. Indeed, some churches and fathers would not even allow such a man to ever be a member of the church again, much less re-enter the pastoral office.

As theologian J. I. Packer points out,

> The fathers' background was the decadent Graeco-Roman culture that had systematically debased marriage and sexual relations for centuries, so perhaps they, too, should not be blamed too much for views such as these [i.e. asceticism and legalism, etc.]. It is obvious, however, that so twisted a record urgently needed to be set straight, and this the Reformers, followed by the Puritans, forthrightly did.[31]

It was in the Reformers and the Puritans, as well as in the life of the church in early America, that we find a recovery of the biblical view of marriage combined with a balanced view of singleness and a deep concern for sexual fidelity. This development came in times of doctrinal reformation and spiritual awakening, both in Europe and in the early colonies.

Two significant conclusions can de deduced from what we have seen in these three eras of church history. First, the church has historically held a very high view of sexual purity in times when it was concerned for faithfulness to revealed truth. Purity was not simply a matter of "being moral" but—and this was especially true in the more balanced eras of the Reformation and early American history—it was a Christian response to the evangel. Men were to love their wives, not because it was good and wise as even pagan philosophers were sometimes prone to see, but because "Christ loved the church and gave

Himself for her." It was out of gospel motive that men kept themselves pure, and it was thus out of gospel motive that men lived separate from the decadence of surrounding culture.

Second, the idea of assigning pastoral ministry to an immoral man would be unthinkable. Such an individual was not "above reproach." Furthermore, the present idea of "restoring" sexually immoral pastors, who have shamefully disqualified themselves, was unknown. If there are any exceptions to this observation they are not readily found nor openly practiced in a manner that would make them commonplace as in our time. The church was willing and able to exercise church discipline when sexual sin revealed itself in the membership, and was especially ready and able to discipline errant pastors. With the Protestant Reformers it was believed that in addition to the presence of the gospel and a right administration of the sacraments, church discipline was a mark of the true church.

What we have seen should be quite obvious. Immoral pastors must be removed from their office, and the evidence points to, in general, permanent disqualification. The penalties might have been excessively harsh, as in the early church's keeping such from the communion for lifetime, but they were certain and swift when such sin brought reproach on the man, his ministry, and his flock.

NOTES

1. D. Martyn Lloyd-Jones, *Expository Sermons on 2 Peter* (Carlisle, Pa.: Banner of Truth, 1983), 140.

2. F. J. Foakes Jackson, *The History of the Christian Church* (Cambridge, England: J. Hall and Son, 1924), 132.

3. Carl A. Volz, *Pastoral Life and Practice in the Early Church* (Minneapolis, Minn.: Augsburg, 1990), 74.

4. Ibid., 74.

5. Ibid., 76–77.

6. Ibid., 77.

7. Ibid., 77.

8. John Bishop, *The Ecclesiastical History of the Second and Third Century, Illustrated from the Writings of Tertullian* (Cambridge, England: J. and J.J. Deighton, 1826), 360.

9. Volz, *Pastoral Life and Practice*, 28, 35.

10. Henry M. Gwatkin, *Selections from Early Christian Writers* (London: MacMillan, 1911), 151.

11. Philip Culbertson and Arthur Shippee, *The Pastor: Readings from the Patristic Period* (Minneapolis, Minn.: Fortress, 1990), 88.

12. Ibid., 49.

13. Ibid., 95.

14. Ibid., 101–102.

15. J. D. Douglas, gen. ed., *The New International Dictionary of the Christian Church* (Grand Rapids, Mich.: Zondervan, 1974), 830.

16. Ulrich Gabler, *Huldrych Zwingli: His Life and Work* (Philadelphia, Pa.: Fortress, 1986), 103–04.

17. Hilton C. Oswald, ed. *Luther's Works*, vol. 28, (St. Louis, Mo.: Concordia, 1973), 284.

18. Steven Ozment, *When Fathers Ruled: Family Life in Reformation Europe* (Cambridge, Mass.: Harvard Univ., 1983), 85.

19. Philip E. Hughes, *The Register of the Company of Pastors in Geneva in the Time of Calvin* (Grand Rapids, Mich.: Eerdmans, 1966), 38–39.

20. Ibid., 39.

21. Ibid., 40.

22. John Calvin, *Commentaries on the Epistles to Timothy, Titus and Philemon* (Grand Rapids, Mich.: Baker, 1979 reprint), 76.

23. John Calvin, *Sermons on the Epistles to Timothy and Titus* (Carlisle, Pa.: Banner of Truth, 1983 facsimile reprint), 1068.

24. Congregational Churches in Massachusetts, *The Cambridge Platform of Church Discipline: Adopted in 1648 and the Confession of Faith* (Boston: Perkins and Whipple, 1850), 61.

25. Cotton Mather, *Brethren Dwelling Together in Unity* (Boston: n.p., 1718), 19.

26. Samuel Cooper, *A Sermon Preached April 9, 1760, at the Ordination of Mr. Joseph Jackson* (Boston: S. Kneeland and T. Green, 1739), 34.

27. In another ordination sermon, Jedediah Morse warns of the dangers of a lax and immoral life destroying a man's effectiveness and his otherwise doctrinally sound ministry. He cautioned that pastors "may possess knowledge without morals. The good they do by their learning will be undone by their vices."

28. John Callender, *A Sermon Preached at the Ordination of Mr. Jeremiah Condy* (Boston: Kneeland and Green, 1739), 15.

29. Andrew Eliot, *A Sermon Preached at the Ordination of the Reverend Mr. Joseph Roberts* (Boston: D. Fowle, 1754), 32.

30. Cotton and Increase Mather, *A Warning to the Flocks Against Wolves in Sheep's Clothing* (Boston: Green and Allen, 1770), 15.

31. J. I. Packer, *A Quest for Godliness* (Wheaton, Ill.: Crossway, 1990), 261.

CHAPTER EIGHT

THE CASE FOR PASTORAL REMOVAL

He who is required by the necessity of his position to speak the highest things is compelled by the same necessity to exemplify the highest things.

Gregory the Great (540–604)

*T*here is a serious danger, especially in devoting an entire book to this matter, that we exaggerate the danger of the present problem, thus drawing undue attention to it. However, an equal danger exists that we ignore a full-scale moral and spiritual epidemic that threatens the health of our churches and has already ruined countless lives. I am convinced that the latter concern is the greater at this time.

Articles, monographs, and whole books have been written on this matter. The debate rages openly on the problems associated with pastoral sexual misconduct. The general assumption, stated or otherwise, is that fallen pastors can and should be fully restored to pastoral office. Some would express this in terms that associate forgiveness with restoration. Others associate restoration with a particular understanding of Galatians 6:1. They argue that we must "restore" to office when the evidence of repentance is real and the fallen leader's own life is genuinely "put back together" after some period of time. We saw in chapter 2 that the general trend today is to restore fairly soon. Sometimes a few years out of ministry is encouraged. Beyond reasonable doubt, however, restoration to office has become the prevalent pattern. Most denominational and church policies assume it and promote it.

HOW PURE MUST A PASTOR BE?

Even when restoration is allowed, one nagging question remains: "How pure must a pastor really be in order to return to ministry?" We know that he is a sinner, like the rest of us. But to be restored we need to be assured that he is a man of integrity, a man of proven and tested character. How are we to view this in actual practice?

Four ministers responded to this question in a *Leadership* interview in 1988. As noted in chapter 2, page 44, Donald Njaa reported that his evangelical denomination has adopted rules that "say we're to be restorative if possible." According to Njaa, "Almost every year we [the denomination] put people back into ministry who were taken out for two to three years." Pastor Charles Swindoll, now president of Dallas Theological Seminary, argued that a person's character becomes seriously flawed through sexual failure. He termed the issue not one of forgiveness but "a matter of the person's lacking the substance required of that office." To this Eugene Peterson replied, "I hear what Chuck is saying, but I guess my basic feeling is that there's nothing that disqualifies us from ministry. Everything is redeemable."

The panel agreed that some high profile men are not likely to ever hold high profile office again, and some men might need to take an "out-of-the-way church," but three of the four participants believed men fundamentally can and should be restored to pastoral ministry if at all possible.[1]

In early 1993 *Christianity Today* reported that a number of denominations had developed clergy misconduct policies with regard to sexual immorality and abuse. Those written procedures ranged from a code of ethics requiring some to be defrocked while others were to be placed on a probationary status with steps for rehabilitation and restoration. Some included policy initiatives on training and prevention while others established funds to help the victims. Most of those policies remain in effect. John Martinson, president of the American Association of Pastoral Counselors, notes that "There are some examples where denominational policies make their way into local churches. On the other hand, there are also examples of churches that better deal with the issue than the synod or other official body—there's a broad continuum." (What is troubling to me is that the evangelical denominations have been perhaps the slowest to respond to this problem.)[2]

But many lay people and some pastors wonder: Is it sound and desirable to begin the restoration of a sexually fallen pastor to office immediately, or even after a year or two? Would time and professional counseling make the difference? If the pastor has disqualified himself, at least for the present time, how long should this disqualification last?

REMOVAL FROM PASTORAL OFFICE

First, it should be plainly understood that the sexually fallen pastor needs to be removed from his office immediately. "That such elders [i.e., those who fall sexually, etc.] should be allowed to retain their office is rather incredible," Lenski comments.[3] This much is still agreed upon by large numbers. Pastors who fall morally must be immediately removed from their office, either by their own resignation or by church discipline if that is necessary. Depending upon the doctrinal tradition of the local church, this will be done in different ways.

I submit that the man's ordination should be rescinded through the same kind of formal channels that were exercised in granting him this originally. In a congregationally governed church this would involve convening a council to investigate the charges and to recommend that the church discipline the man if the evidence supports this action. In other systems of government a clear path for such action is usually already established in a book of order, or in an adopted policy manual for the fellowship.

Ordaining bodies and related documents should state much more clearly that should the pastor discredit himself through any scandalous sin, such as becoming "disqualified" through sexual promiscuity, he would willingly give up his ordination. If he will not submit to this he should not be ordained, since he fails to understand the gravity of either his call or the office he is about to enter. And if he will not surrender his ordination, then it must be taken away through proper church procedure.

As I hope it is apparent by now, the potential for later restoration to pastoral office and ministry should be seriously doubted. The sexually fallen pastor might find new venues for Christian service that will be extremely encouraging to him and others. Indeed, in time he should be encouraged, like all members of the church, to use his gifts in the service of others. But the use of teaching gifts is never synonymous with being a pastor in the New Testament.

What must be challenged in our present practice is not a man's restoration to God, nor his restoration to wife and family. He may even be restored to the church, though this will be a difficult process because of the response of a diverse membership. He will probably need to leave the particular church that he has pastored because of the damage which has been done and the recovery that needs to begin under new leadership. (His ultimate restoration to the visible church, which remains the goal, will certainly involve his staying in touch with his former church. This might well be done through a formal "restoration" council of capable leaders. In due season the success of this can hopefully be rejoiced in by the entire congregation.)

However, we must challenge the idea that, in most cases, he can requalify for pastoral ministry. The facts argued in previous chapters that certain behavior, and particularly sexually sinful behavior, creates a total violation of trust that disqualifies a person from future ministry as a pastor. While it is appropriate to acknowledge the sinfulness of all men, and the struggles with temptation that every pastor faces, a pastor who falls into sexual sin, under most circumstances, has permanently disqualified himself from the pulpit.

By *disqualified*, I mean simply, "rendered unfit for office." This does not mean the man is lost, useless, or "on the shelf" for service to Christ. What is particularly troublesome about most arguments against disqualification is how they view the pastorate in the first place. One tends to get the idea, from reading some of these arguments, that pastors have a right to their office.

Augustine (354–430), the famous North African bishop, spoke well when he said: "For you, I am bishop, but with you, I am a Christian. The first is an office accepted, the second a grace received; one a danger, the other safety. If then I am gladder by far to be redeemed with you than I am to be placed over you, I shall, as the Lord commanded, be more completely your servant."[4]

Clement of Rome (ca. 30–100) was a pastor who understood that certain sin might bring a pastor to the place where he could no longer serve the church in the place he had been given. He wrote: "Blessed are the presbyters who have gone before in the way, who came to a fruitful and perfect end; for they need have no fear lest anyone depose them from their assigned place."

TWO OBJECTIONS

Don't Ignore the God-Given Gift

But today it is frequently argued, "The church needs this gifted pastor. If you disqualify an adulterous pastor, as a matter of general policy or approach to this sin, then you deny the church of some of her most gifted and needed leadership."

This kind of argument seems to be advanced in the reasoning of several noted evangelical leaders in our time. Kenneth Kantzer writes, "I know of fallen leaders who long to return to the kind of spiritual ministry they previously enjoyed, but no evangelical congregations will accept them. Their gifts of leadership are permanently lost to the church."[5]

Such thinking lies at the heart of the restoration of Pastor David Hocking to ministry. As discussed in chapter 2, Pastor Chuck Smith of nearby Calvary Chapel defended his invitation to David Hocking to minister to the Costa Mesa congregation only weeks after his moral failure was publicly revealed by saying, "This man is a gifted Bible teacher, and if he doesn't resume his teaching, I'm afraid he'll be literally and totally destroyed."

I believe that response takes the ministry of the gospel and the call of God far too lightly. Furthermore, it takes ministers and their importance as gifted teachers far too seriously. Surely no one would have the temerity to argue that God needs us—or that without us something will be lacking in His kingdom's work.

> *THE CHURCH WOULD BE MUCH STRONGER WITHOUT ITS FALLEN LEADERS BACK IN POSITIONS OF AUTHORITY. INDEED, THE CHURCH SUFFERS PRECISELY BECAUSE SHE HAS COMPROMISED HER MORAL INTEGRITY.*

To the contrary, the church would be much stronger without its fallen leaders back in positions of authority. Indeed, the church suffers precisely because she has compromised her moral integrity. This invites the discipline of God upon the church. When leadership breaks down, all pastors are affected in one sense. Witness the present confusion and mistrust of the Roman Catholic Church across the U.S. raised by its earlier practice of moving sexually abusive priests from place to place, covering their sin and seeking to keep them and their gifts in the church.

A. W. Tozer has reminded us that God is never in a "must-have" situation when it comes to pastors:

> God wants worshipers before workers; indeed the only acceptable workers are those who have learned the lost art of worship. It is inconceivable that a sovereign and holy God should be so hard up for workers that he would press into service anyone who had been empowered regardless of his moral qualifications. The very stones would praise Him if the need arose and a thousand legions of angels would leap to do His will. Gifts and power for service the Spirit surely desires to impart; but holiness and spiritual worship come first. [6]

Benefit from the "Wounded Healer"

Still others advance the previously mentioned idea that fallen pastors can become "wounded healers." What is generally meant is that men who have suffered deep pain through moral failure can more effectively minister out of their newly discovered weakness. They are presumably better able to sympathize and help others, so the argument says.

Kantzer expresses something of the thinking of this approach when he writes:

> Paradoxically, God sometimes permits us to fall into sin for our own growth and sanctification and ministry. Executive placement officer Robert W. Dingman reminds us: "Before Bathsheba caught his attention, King David would have delighted the search committee, but later he was clearly 'damaged goods.' I submit that he was a much better candidate after Bathsheba, as was Peter after the agonizing over his denials of Christ. People who have experienced the penalties of error have often received an inoculation that gives a future immunity. Should these truths be ignored by those who choose our leaders?"[7]

Later Kantzer added, "Often our decision becomes a delicate balance between a judgment as to the genuineness of the person's repentance and a quite different judgment as to *what the fallen leader has learned from this experience that will enable him or her to do a better job* and to be preserved from falling into a similar error" (emphasis mine). Kantzer cited three biblical leaders who became stronger after their repentance. "With true remorse the guilty person will have learned from his fall and be the stronger for it. This was true of David, Peter, and Paul."[8]

This is readily accepted in the present environment because it sounds so much like grace, when evangelicals have tended toward legalism for so long. But it can readily lead to what Dietrich Bonhoeffer called "cheap grace." It has helped to produce the "wounded healer" idea. However, we must remember that a man's pastoral ministry is a gift given by the church, and it can surely be taken back by the church if the individual is no longer qualified to hold it.

If, as argued in chapters 5 and 6, the pastor must be qualified to hold office, then he must remain qualified to continue
in it. The trust he has been given can be taken away. This
should not even be debated if we are serious about the New
Testament. What is debatable is this: Can a man become disqualified? For how long? For a long time, beyond the modern
policies of one to three years?

THE CASE FOR COMPLETE DISQUALIFICATION

From all that we have seen it seems reasonable that sexual
sin disqualifies a pastor from future ministry. This seems to be
true precisely because of the gravity of the offense, the person
in whom the sin was committed, and the high nature of ministerial calling itself.

All sin is deceitful and potentially destructive of pastoral
ministry. What I am arguing for is this: sexual sin is especially
able to deceive, to harden the heart and to bring untold harm
and destruction to those touched by it (cf. 1 Corinthians 6:18–
20); thus it destroys pastoral leadership whenever it occurs. It
is a fire of destruction that burns scores of people when it occurs in the life of one chosen to shepherd the flock of Christ. It
nurtures the cynicism of the world, since the fallen pastor can
no longer have a "good reputation with those outside," and it
destroys trust within the church by making the man no longer
"above reproach" or "blameless."

This needs to be further developed in the light of our present crisis and the confusion that exists in the church at large.

ARGUMENTS FOR RESTORATION
TO PASTORAL MINISTRY

Several popular arguments favor restoring a sexually fallen
pastor to the pastorate. Some of these arguments have already
been addressed in previous chapters but should be mentioned.

God's Forgiveness

First, there is the argument that since God forgives all sin upon repentance, then we must forgive and this means restoration to office.

That God forgives is not the issue, as we will see more clearly in chapter 10. He does forgive genuinely repentant sinners who trust Him. I do fear that forgiveness is often taken in a rather cavalier manner by many who seem to think that "My role is sinning and God's role is forgiving!" The rampant antinomianism ("lawlessness") of much modern Christianity should cause us to be very cautious with any approach that treats forgiveness lightly.

Second, it is argued that several biblical texts and personal human examples actually require us to restore fallen pastors. There are three such texts that are generally used to suggest we must restore to pastoral ministry in order to obey God. We need to consider each of them briefly.

Arguments from Scripture and Responses

First, let's look again at one common text used to argue on behalf of restoration, Galatians 6:1. We have considered it briefly; now let's investigate it in depth. Paul instructs the church at Galatia, and he tells all believers: "Brethren, even if a man is caught in any trespass, you who are spiritual, restore such a one in a spirit of godliness, each one looking to yourself, lest you too be tempted."

This passage, you may recall, was cited by Calvary Chapel leadership in restoring David Hocking. However, the larger ethical context of this passage concerns restoration to a former spiritual condition of health, i.e., to be "mended" or "restored to a former condition," not to pastoral leadership. As Jay Smith notes in the journal *Bibliotheca Sacra*, "Absent from the context is any indication that Paul was concerned with restoration to leadership. Rehabilitating the sinner, not reinstating the leader, was the primary issue."[9]

Further, the Pauline use of the generic term for "a man" (*anthropos*) used in Galatians 6:1 argues for a general use as well; thus this is not a special text referring to the actual restoring of pastors to their previous office.

That a man can be restored to useful service is not in question. What is seriously in question is restoration to his former ministry, from which he has now been removed due to his violation of the trust established between him and the flock of Christ.

Second, some cite 1 Timothy 5:22 as allowing penitent elders to return to their pastoral ministries. The admonition concerns the laying on of hands: "Do not lay hands upon anyone too hastily and thus share responsibility for the sins of others; keep yourself free from sin."

Some have suggested that this text envisions readmitting penitents into the church, after a moral lapse, once sufficient time has elapsed. Therefore, it would also refer to readmitting penitent elders to their pastoral ministry through the ceremony of the laying on of hands. They add to this the argument that the immediate context, namely verses 19–20, refers to the discipline of pastors.

The problem with this argument is that it can't be reasonably sustained exegetically. First, no evidence, either in the Scripture or in the writings of the Church Fathers, supports the notion that reinstatement to office is in view in the "laying on of hands" referred to here. Both Cyprian and Eusebius refer to readmitting a penitent to the fellowship of the church via "the laying on of hands," but there is no evidence that this is ever applied to restoring elders to office.

Further, the best early evidence indicates that the early church understood this text to refer to original ordination to pastoral office, not to restoration. And finally, references to the "laying on of hands" which appear elsewhere in the pastoral epistles refer to the recognition of special gifts of the Holy Spirit given for one's ministry, not to the restoration of penitent pastors to office.

The conclusion that best explains the context and the extra-biblical evidence we have available is that this verse is "an injunction against a hasty initial ordination." It is a text that

squares up with Paul's previously expressed concern for ordaining men to the office of pastor who have an established
character.[10]

Third, the restoration of Peter is often cited. Here is the
narrative from John 21:15–22:

> So when they had finished breakfast, Jesus said to Simon Peter, "Si-
> mon, son of John, do you love Me more than these?" He said to Him,
> "Yes, Lord; You know that I love You. He said to him, "Tend My
> lambs." He said to him again a second time, "Simon, son of John, do
> you love Me?" He said to Him, "Yes, Lord; You know that I love You."
> He said to him, "Shepherd My sheep." He said to him the third time,
> "Simon, son of John, do you love Me?" Peter was grieved because He
> said to him the third time, "Do you love Me?" And he said to Him,
> "Lord, You know all things; You know that I love You." Jesus said to
> him, "Tend My sheep. Truly, truly, I say to you, when you were young-
> er, you used to gird yourself, and walk wherever you wished; but when
> you grow old, you will stretch out your hands and someone else will
> gird you, and bring you where you do not wish to go." Now this He
> said, signifying by what kind of death he would glorify God. And when
> He had spoken this, He said to him, "Follow Me!" Peter, turning
> around, saw the disciple whom Jesus loved following them, the one
> who also leaned back on His breast at the supper, and said, "Lord, who
> is the one who betrays You?" Peter therefore seeing him, said to Jesus,
> "Lord, and what about this man?" Jesus said to him, "If I want him to
> remain until I come, what is that to you? You follow Me!"

Here we read of Peter's reinstatement by the Lord Jesus
after he had thrice denied Him just days before. It is important to
realize what had happened. Peter had openly cursed the Savior,
saying he never knew Him and denying allegiance to Him. His
failure was great, and his recommissioning in the text in view
is quite significant. This scenario is often cited as evidence that
sexually fallen pastors should also be reinstated to office.

Nonetheless, Peter was not guilty of sexual immorality, so
his case does not specifically line up with what is our present
concern. Nor is he specifically reinstated to the office of pastor,
having previously been examined as to his character and found
being "above reproach."

One argument from this text reasons in the following way.
Peter is the prime example of the grace of reinstatement. His
life of denying Christ with curses (oaths) was the most serious

of failures. And in his reinstatement Jesus commissions him to "shepherd" his sheep. When Peter writes later in his first epistle, he urges pastors to "shepherd" the flock of God (5:2). The same word is used in both texts, thus demonstrating that Peter was reinstated as a shepherd who then exhorts shepherds.

One defender of Peter as the archetype of the restored minister once wrote to me: "How long after Peter's blasphemous denial did Jesus give his ministry back to him? Ten days! And how long after that did Peter preach at Pentecost? Forty days!"

What can we say to these arguments? First, Peter's sin was not in the category of sexual sin (1 Corinthians 6:18); thus it was not "against the body" as argued in chapter 3. Moreover, while it was a "character sin," it clearly did not entail the willful hypocrisy, cavalier deception, and gross perpetual disobedience that goes with adultery. Peter had followed Jesus, with deep feeling and determination to obey, into Caiphas' courtyard. He was there because he loved Jesus. His failure was not thought out. It was not a series of steps leading up to a colossal and planned sin. He was, as we might say, "blindsided." When men who commit adultery argue that this is what happened to them, the hope of real repentance and meaningful recovery is seriously in doubt.

Further, this approach in using Peter raises the issue of the normativeness of using biblical narrative to establish faith and practice in the church. It is a hermeneutical principle fraught with serious complications. Issues such as Peter's unique place among the Twelve (he was a part of three chosen ones from the larger group), Jesus' personal involvement in this whole scenario, His own relationship to the man Simon Peter, and the occurrence of these events before Pentecost must all be factored into the consideration of this account.

I suggest that Peter's restoration (to office as an apostle) would best be seen as a very wonderful exception, but not a specific pattern. Exceptions, properly viewed, generally prove a rule. The norm is that this scenario does not apply to the larger question before us in this chapter.

The Argument of David's Adultery

The story of King David's sexual fall is well-known. The sin was both heinous and aggravated, for David was both an adulterer and a murderer. God specifically called him to account through the prophet Nathan. The king then repented openly of his sin according to Psalm 51 and Psalm 32. He was not removed from his office, even for a brief period of time.

As a friend remarked to me, "David's two offices [sic] were teaching and evangelism (Psalm 51:13)." Later he added, "Whom did God reinstate so as to be used as a holy instrument to write Holy Scripture? David, the deceiver, conniver, liar, and adulterer." And as mentioned in chapter 2, churches have defended pastoral restoration based on "how fully God restored David."

The hermeneutical and ethical conclusions of such thinking are replete with serious problems, not to mention dangerous implications for the church under the New Covenant. David was a middle-eastern, polygamous potentate, not a priest serving God's people in sacred worship and leadership through the sanctuary. I realize that there is not a one-for-one relationship between the priest and the New Covenant pastor (as seen earlier), but neither is a one-for-one comparison to be made between a potentate in Israel and a pastor either.

To make David's tragic fall and continued reign as king a pattern for "pastoral restoration to office" under the New Covenant (which has specifically revealed character requirements for those who would hold office) is to make a quantum leap from the context of the Old Testament account. David's son Solomon was called "the preacher," but does his life serve as a specific model for New Covenant preachers?

David was forgiven, make no doubt about it. This is the marvelous truth that transcends the covenant itself. But what is also apparent is that the sword never left his house. From the time of his fall, his reign knew nothing but bloodshed and grief.

Despite David's laudable and true repentance, his reign went downhill. The terrible facts are these: his baby died; his beautiful daughter, Tamar, was raped by her half-brother Amnon; Amnon was murdered by Tamar's full brother Absalom; Absalom so came to hate his father David for his moral turpitude that he led a rebellion under the tutelage of Bathsheba's resentful grandfather, Ahithophel. His throne lost its glory and the great blessing of God was removed. The crown may have remained, but the stability and unity were gone.

If we must insist on citing David's sin as a case for pastoral restoration to office then I think we should at least get the story right and warn both fallen pastors and churches of the full implications of this account.

Other examples are sometimes cited, but each one has less evidence to support it than the ones considered above. And each can be handled in ways that parallel what we have seen above. Either the sin was in a category that does not parallel the problem presently before us, the person involved was not an elder in the church of Jesus Christ, or the hermeneutical principle behind the argument will simply not hold up under more careful scrutiny.

WHAT'S THE ANSWER?

No sure biblical text supplies indisputable evidence for restoration to the pastorate after the fall into sexual sin. But by the same token, no text directly argues for permanent disqualification. So what's the answer? Can we argue with confidence for one position over another? Yes, for a variety of reasons to be discussed in the next chapter, we can find permanent disqualification from pastoral ministry the norm (with a few exceptions) for the pastor who yields to sexual sin. Let's proceed to the heart of the matter.

NOTES

1. "How Pure Must a Pastor Be?", *Leadership*, 9:2 (Spring 1988), 16–17.

2. "Coping with Sexual Misconduct in the Church," *Christianity Today*, 11 January 1993, 48.

3. R. C. H. Lenski, *The Interpretation of St. Paul's Epistles to the Colossians, to the Thessalonians, to Timothy, to Titus and to Philemon* (Minneapolis, Minn.: Augsburg, 1937), 685.

4. From "Pastoring through the Ages," a one-page listing of notable statements about ministry by early church fathers through contemporary preachers, collected by the editors of *Leadership* magazine (Chrtistianity Today, Inc., Carol Stream, Ill.)

5. Kenneth S. Kantzer, "The Road to Restoration," *Christianity Today,* 20 November 1987, 19.

6. A. W. Tozer, *That Incredible Christian* (Harrisburg, Pa.: Christian Publications, 1964), 37.

7. Ibid., 20.

8. Ibid., 21, 22.

9. Jay E. Smith, "Can Fallen Leaders Be Restored to Leadership?" *Bibliotheca Sacra* 151 (October–December, 1994), 468.

10. Ibid., 469-70.

CHAPTER NINE

THE HEART
OF THE MATTER

Private men indeed sin; but in pastors there is blame of
negligence; and still more, when they deviate even the least from
the right way, a greater offense is given.

John Calvin

*T*ry as we might, when answering the question "Should fallen
pastors be restored?" we cannot prove a position by exegesis of
a Bible passage in a manner that can satisfy all Christians. I do
not expect discussion of this question to go away because of the
arguments I am offering. I hope the arguments of previous
chapters and their summary here might at least add a measure
of more careful ethical practice to the present scene, where
sexually fallen pastors are encouraged to return to pastoral
ministry so quickly.

We now look at the heart of the matter—what churches
should do when their pastors succumb to sexual sin. The three
choices mentioned in chapter 2 still stand: immediate restoration to the pastoral office, restoration to office after the passage
of time, or restoration of the pastor without restoration to his
former office.

A TRAGIC PURSUIT

Whatever course of action we choose, I advise caution. Some churches and ministries actually pursue the service of fallen men. This is tragic. Typically the churches believe the popular idea that the fallen man will bring to the church a new compassion due to their experience—the "wounded healer" idea. But consider the ramifications of such thinking for those thousands of lesser known brothers, whose gifts might well be less prominent, yet whose lives remain chaste and blameless. We are in danger of creating a new kind of "care-giver," namely the "fallen brother" who supposedly can help adulterers and the sexually immoral precisely because he has been there. Does such a care-giver really understand this sin better than a pastor who has never been personally involved?

Remember that the Savior is able to "sympathize with us in our weaknesses, yet he was without sin" (Hebrews 4:15). As Jesus told the apostle Paul, "My grace is sufficient for you, for power is perfected in weakness." In response, Paul accepted his shortcomings, writing, "Most gladly, therefore, I will rather boast about my weaknesses, that the power of Christ may dwell in me" (2 Corinthians 12:9). Brokenness and weakness are qualities that truly empower New Covenant ministry. In great measure they are missing in much of what today is seen in public ministry; let us never think that they will be uniquely discovered via the way of sexual adultery. Such sin does not specifically qualify a man for pastoral ministry.

SIX REASONS FOR CAUTION

Here is the heart of the matter: I believe the pastor should not seek nor should the church leadership advise restoration to office. There are a number of reasons for this recommendation, most of which have been either fully developed or mentioned already. Here is a summary of each.

1. The Pastor's High Calling

Under the New Covenant, the pastor/elder has a high calling indeed. The office of pastor ("overseer") itself is one which requires the qualities cited in 1 Timothy 3 and Titus 1. That the entire congregation should be "above reproach" seems self-evident, but the elder *"must* be above reproach" [emphasis added].

There is no exception for him. Why? His office is that of an undershepherd who will care for the souls of those for whom Christ died. He must tend to the lives of people who sin, who repent and who need his help, both through a consistent life and in his faithful teaching of sound doctrine.

2. The Pastor As a Public Figure

The pastor is a very public figure, whose life must be an example for all to see and follow. Thus when his public example is destroyed by sexual sin, his life will never be the same as regarding public persona.

This is in view in the requirement that his family and marriage be in order and that outsiders believe him to have a "good reputation" (1 Timothy 3:7). The world will judge the church by its ministers, whether we like it or not.

3. A Possible Relapse

The distinct possibility exists that this man may fall again. Sadly, there is an overabundance of such cases.

The patterns of sexual sin are not easily broken. Most of the cases we have read about in public accounts are of those who have fallen more than once. In addition, the discovery of the sin is usually not made known because the pastor confesses it, but rather because he was exposed or caught.

All of this merely underscores the devious nature of this sin. It is a sin that is almost never alone. It brings a host of other sins with it: lying, deceit, and hypocrisy. The blatant personal deception that frequently attends this sin must be recognized honestly. When men "cover up" for so long, they will, by

virtue of their patterns, "sear their conscience" in some manner. They make a kind of peace treaty with sin on a level that
destroys the true knowledge of God and of self.

4. The Pastor As a Model

Concerning the lifestyle of the "man of God," the New Testament consistently emphasizes the minister's character and
lifestyle. He is to be a model of integrity.

The pastor who has not lived consistently with his calling
and position cannot rule the church of God in love and with
integrity. Aelred (1109–67) wrote: "Since you [O Lord] have
appointed this blind guide to lead [your people], for their
sakes, Lord, if not for mine, teach him whom you have made to
be their teacher; lead him whom you have bidden to lead them;
rule him who is their ruler."

The one who has not been consistently led in the paths of
righteousness by the Holy Spirit cannot lead others in paths he
has not followed. Some kinds of sin, as we have argued already,
irreparably shatter a man's life and reputation and thus disqualify him from being a consistent model for the church.

"Where did we get the idea that a year's leave of absence
can restore integrity to a man who has squandered his reputation and destroyed people's trust? Certainly not from the Bible," argues John MacArthur. "Trust forfeited is not so easily
regained. Once purity is sacrificed, the ability to lead by example is gone forever."[1]

Integrity is essential to the ministry of a pastor. Biblically,
integrity means wholeness or consistent, universal obedience.
You do what God commands and avoid what He forbids. And
you do it based upon the love of Christ revealed in the gospel.
MacArthur emphasizes the matter of integrity when he adds,
"Hideous or scandalous sin leaves a reproach that cannot be
blotted out. The persistent memory of betrayal made public
leaves such a man unable to stand blameless before people and
lead them spiritually."[2]

5. A Lack of Judgment

The sin of sexual immorality in a pastor displays a complete lack of judgment and discernment.

Paul prayed for good judgment by the Philippian believers. "And this I pray, that your love may abound still more and more in real knowledge and all discernment, so that you may approve the things that are excellent in order to be sincere and blameless until the day of Christ" (Philippians 1:9–10). The apostle wanted such discernment for every member of this congregation. Surely good judgment must find life and expression through the example of the pastor(s).

A man who has allowed himself to slip into sexual sin demonstrates poor judgment. How can a man who lacks good judgment lead and shepherd the flock of God when, after extensive examination for such leadership, he is now found to be completely lacking in good sense, both morally and ethically?

6. A Stricter Judgment

A stricter judgment must be consistently exercised in regard to the one who leads and teaches the church. This seems to me to be self-evident in light of both James 3:1 and Luke 12:48b. But should the church judge such men when they fall? I answer, "Positively!"

But why? The answer of the New Testament is that we can and must judge our pastors. Paul writes to the Corinthians: "What business is it of mine to judge those outside the church? Are you not to judge those inside? God will judge those outside. 'Expel the wicked man from among you'" (1 Corinthians 5:1–13; NIV). Here Paul speaks of a responsibility all have for one another. And he goes on to urge serious and careful "self-judgment" (11:27–33). In my estimation, we need to circumspectly hear the general principle expressed in the words, "For it is time for judgment to begin with the family of God" (1 Peter 4:17a).

God will judge us, especially if we do not judge ourselves as He has told us to do.

THE WELFARE OF THE CHURCH

As has been mentioned before, the reproach of adultery will never leave the man who falls, even if his repentance is proven over the years that follow (Proverbs 6:32–33). For this reason we must come to grips with the concerns of those who cannot accept returning fallen pastors to leadership. Those who question the return of a sexually fallen pastor are not generally "legalists" who have a hang-up regarding grace. They are more often conscientious church members who are concerned for the welfare of their church.

In his fair-minded and irenic book *If Ministers Fall, Can They Be Restored?*, Tim LaHaye argues that fallen ministers can be restored to office. He adds a caution, though.

> While I believe that the Scripture teaches that a fallen minister can be restored to ministry, I do not believe all fallen ministers should be restored. All ministers are different, and circumstances surrounding their sexual sin vary radically. Each minister should be evaluated individually . . . by a group of spiritually mature men who have known the minister well for many years.[3]

LaHaye gives an illustration of a man who committed sexual sin over a period of several weeks. He repented and received help from a godly fellow elder. His ministry seemed to flourish for over a decade afterward. Then his past, supposedly forgotten, leaked out, destroying his present ministry completely. The way of the transgressor is hard (Proverbs 13:15), observed LaHaye, no matter how we deal with the sin.

Ideally, one might wish that the modern approach would work, but in the real world of tragedies and shattered lives it usually does not. I think it does not precisely because it should not! What interests me is that LaHaye, who is so honest in his approach, admits that in his own survey he has found that almost all of the godly women he questioned would be glad to forgive their pastor if he fell morally. When he asked these same women if they would want this man to be their pastor, 90 percent said no![4] I find this astounding, but not at all surprising. I submit that these godly women know something that we should all listen to more carefully.

"When a minister desecrates his position by sexual indiscretion, he can never again regain his former status of integrity," LaHaye wrote. "God may use him in some form of ministry after a significant waiting period, but I do not believe he will ever achieve the heights he may have reached if he had not sinned sexually. He will always be a former adulterer. Even *forgiveness* will not change that in the eyes of man" (emphasis added).[5]

One can understand why these sisters have trouble with a fallen man still being their pastor because of their deep concern for their families. They find it difficult to trust this man. And for good reason. The fact is this: The reproach will not be wiped away!

A long-term restoration process can bring about the kind of Christian compassion and help that may very well restore the fallen man's marriage and family life. However, I seriously doubt he can ever have the same relationships with his church family again. The trust he has thrown away will never be fully regained. Even when men have remained in a local church, or have returned to it after a previous fall, the number of those who cannot trust him is always significantly high, with many spiritual casualties being the result of his restoration to public ministry.

Is the problem simply location? Can a move to another place change all of this? The answers to questions like these are mixed, and evidence does not seem to support the conclusion that simply changing churches will allow the fallen pastor to return to pastoral ministry easily.

MAY HE EVER RETURN?

The question is still asked, "Does God plainly forbid all sexually fallen pastors from ever, under any circumstances, re-entering the office of pastor?" As has been stated already, the general principle should be that men should not seek to re-enter the office of pastor, and if they do the church must know fully of their past and its resulting implications. But "does God plainly forbid it?"

I answer: As we have seen, no text makes it imperative that we must seek the restoration of the fallen pastor to office, and no text plainly forbids it either. Does this mean we are left in the dark? Are we groping about with no response to this immensely divisive question? I think not, in the light of the ethical approach we have taken. I believe we must conclude that the church should not make a general or procedural practice of restoring sexually fallen ministers, at least not for the foreseeable future. Any exception should be viewed as establishing the general principle. The pattern needs to be reclaimed that was practiced in earlier eras of church history. The modern practice needs to be corrected dramatically and as soon as possible.

This issue may well be a watershed for many of our churches, but it may also become a place where reformation begins in new and powerful ways.

WHAT ABOUT FUTURE MINISTRY?

But what should we do with the fallen pastor regarding his future ministry opportunities? The local church body can help in two ways: recovery and adjustment, and restoration to an alternate ministry.

Help the Former Pastor Deal with Sudden Change

When the pastor has sinned morally and is removed from his position, his professional career—one he has known for perhaps many years—has come to a sudden and terrible end. This problem, though not totally unique to pastors, raises different concerns that most men will never face.

When the pastor confesses his sexual misconduct, he is out of work, has no salary, and has little or no prospect of getting a good job soon. He may very well need training for the development of a new vocation, as well as temporary help in providing for the needs of his family. Many churches have not done well in addressing these concerns.

One minister who resigned his pastoral position due to an admitted indiscretion allowed another pastor, Ed Dobson, to helpfully recount his story of failure and what followed. The fallen pastor told Dobson,

> The greatest pressure when you step out of ministry . . . is figuring out how to earn a living. You discover very quickly that the world out there is very unimpressed that you've been a pastor. You're essentially qualified to do nothing. The skills of ministry don't necessarily transfer into business.[6]

If the church is committed to helping those who are weak and who show repentance, then it must get involved in ways that are both appropriate and loving. Could the church not set up a committee for personal recovery which includes oversight of the man's restoration process, as well as genuine involvement in helping the pastor and his family financially until work can be found? Severance pay can help in the first few months but in the long term the man needs to be equipped for meaningful labor that will allow him to rebuild his own life.

One minister who has investigated this issue thoroughly during his seminary research came to this important conclusion:

> The decision to restore the pastor is not elective; rather, it is an obligation, but one that carries serious repercussions. The fallen man's spiritual life and marital relationship will require huge sacrifices of time by the [restoration] committee. Those overseeing the healing must be committed to seeing the individual fully restored to his wife, church, and Lord.
>
> One component that underpins this whole discussion is that time must not be a factor. The rebuilding of a life cannot be placed on a schedule as one might in the construction of a new building. To err by setting a time limit could lead to the release of someone from discipline just as the process was approaching a substantive breakthrough. Until the individual attains spiritual stability and marital intimacy, the committee has not finished its business.[7]

Restore to Alternate Ministry

But assuming that the former pastor has put his life back in order and has addressed the failures that were manifest in his moral collapse, what next? Should he begin to plan to re-

turn to pastoral ministry as part of his recovery process? Generally, no. And it is precisely here that major errors are frequently
being made in the modern approach. We will look at some of the
arguments surrounding this issue in another chapter.

What should he do regarding his gifts? His responsibility
to serve the Lord faithfully?

He should make himself available, quietly and unobtrusi-
vely, to be used as the Lord might allow, but he is best advised
to not pursue pastoral leadership or the office of elder. He
should pursue some alternative ministry.

The apostle Paul makes it very clear that those who shepherd the flock as pastors/elders *must be above moral lapses
that hinder the care of the flock or ministry to the community*. (See especially 1 Timothy 3:2, 7 and Titus 1:6–9.) The same
should be true of godly and properly qualified deacons, according to 1 Timothy 3:8–13.

---

*FORMER PASTORS WHO HAVE FALLEN MIGHT
WELL SERVE THE CHURCH IN . . . VIRTUALLY
ANY CAPACITY . . . EXCEPT PASTORAL
MINISTRIES THAT ARE CLEARLY ASSOCIATED
WITH THE DIRECT SHEPHERDING OF THE
FLOCK AND ITS OVERSIGHT.*

In practice, this can mean that former pastors who have
fallen might well serve the church in various capacities. Those
capacities might (but not necessarily) include virtually any capacity in the church except pastoral ministries that are clearly
associated with the direct shepherding of the flock and its oversight.[8] Churches may well vary in their understanding of this
matter, and much wisdom is needed in applying the principle
to each local situation.

A WORD FROM SPURGEON

For many years the thought and insight of the great nine-teenth-century preacher/pastor Charles Haddon Spurgeon have influenced and powerfully shaped my own life. In his wise and often straightforward style he has summarized the issues well. The following comments, taken from his classic book *Lectures to My Students*, state my own position in a general way (though a few phrases leave me in a bit of doubt about all he means). I will let him have the last word on this matter of pastoral restoration to the pulpit.

> The highest moral character must be [diligently] maintained. Many are disqualified for office in the church who are well enough as simple members. I hold very stern opinions with regard to Christian men who have fallen into gross sin; I rejoice that they may be truly converted, and may be with mingled hope and caution received into the church; but I question, gravely question whether a man who has grossly sinned should be very readily restored to the pulpit. As John Angell James remarks, "When a preacher of righteousness has stood in the way of sinners, he should never again open his lips in the great congregation until his repentance is as notorious as his sin." . . . Alas! The beard of reputation once shorn is hard to grow again. Open immorality, in most cases, however deep the repentance, is a fatal sign that ministerial graces were never in the man's character. . . . There must be no ugly rumours as to ministerial inconsistency in the past, or the hope of usefulness will be slender. Into the church such fallen ones are to be received as penitents, and into the ministry they may be received if God puts them there; my doubt is not about that, but as to whether God ever did place them there; and my belief is that we should be very slow to help back to the pulpit men, who having been once tried, have proved themselves to have far too little grace to stand the crucial test of ministerial life.[9]

NOTES:

1. As quoted in Tim LaHaye, *If Ministers Fall, Can They Be Restored?* (Grand Rapids, Mich.: Zondervan, 1990), 149.

2. Ibid., 149–50.

3. Ibid., 162.

4. Ibid., 165.

5. Ibid., 164.

6. Ed Dobson, "Restoring a Fallen Colleague," *Leadership* (Winter 1992), 118.

7. James Boyd Newton, "Pastoral Immorality: Grounds for Permanent Disqualification," a D. Min. writing project, Temple Baptist Seminary, 1993, 73–74.

8. The case of David Hocking is discussed in chapter 2; Hocking was placed in a teaching and speaking ministry at another southern California church by its pastor, Chuck Smith. In this instance, the concern is that Hocking received public pastoral responsibilities: he was allowed to preach to the church body, teach men in training for ministry, and, in general, assist in the overall care of this large, highly regarded church. I am not sure whether the church considers David Hocking formally to be a pastor; yet in practice Hocking is pastoring thousands of people weekly and leading conference ministry widely, all because of the view expressed in chapter 2. I believe such action by Smith and the ministry that has followed the action is problematic for the church.

9. Charles H. Spurgeon, *Lectures to My Students* (Pasadena, Tex.: Pilgrim Publications, 1881, 1990 reprint), 8–9.

CHAPTER TEN

HOW SHALL
WE RESTORE
THE FALLEN MAN?

The value of time in the process of healing and restoration is that it permits grace to have its effect upon the soul and spirit of the fallen man. In my own case, the magnificence of grace has been magnified over time and allowed me to see the sheer undeservedness of it, my inability to hear it and God's consistent willingness to impart it.

A Fallen Pastor

*R*egardless of how we answer all of the difficult questions related to disqualification, spiritual leaders of the church must lovingly enter into a painful process of personal restoration for their fallen pastor. One cannot seriously doubt this admonition in light of Paul's counsel: "If a man is caught in any trespass, you who are spiritual, restore such a one in a spirit of gentleness" (Galatians 6:1).

But how are we to do this? What is involved? To what are we to restore the fallen pastor? When should the process begin? How are we to go about this taxing, but crucial, labor?

RESTORATION DEFINED

First, let's be sure we understand the meaning of the term *restoration*. The concept of restoration is discussed almost endlessly in our day. Many have concluded that restoration means that any person who sins has the *right* to full service in his former ministry as long as he or she confesses and asks for restoration.

In this kind of thinking, there are no lasting consequences. The assumption seems to be that restoration at all levels is always possible. I seriously question this. Let me explain.

Restoration is the actual act of restoring, which is the verbal form of a Latin word meaning "to bring back to use, or to the original state." Indeed, one definition given in Webster's New Riverside Dictionary (1984) is "to put someone back in a former position." The illustration given is that of restoring a deposed monarch to his throne.

HE MAY BE RESTORED TO HIS WIFE, BUT HIS MARRIAGE WILL NEVER BE THE SAME, NO MATTER WHAT RESTORATION MEANS. FURTHER, . . . CAN WE EVER IMAGINE THAT HE WILL BE FULLY RESTORED TO THE TRUST, INTEGRITY, AND CONFIDENCE HE MOST LIKELY ENJOYED PREVIOUS TO HIS SCANDALOUS BEHAVIOR?

When we speak of restoring a fallen pastor we then must ask, how and to what? Can he be *fully* restored? A moment's thought reveals that plainly he can never be fully restored, if by this we mean put back into the place he was before the fall. He may be restored to his wife, but his marriage will never be the same, no matter what restoration means. Further, his church, denomination, or ministry may restore him to the office of pastor, but can we ever imagine that he will be fully restored to the trust, integrity, and confidence he most likely enjoyed previous to his scandalous behavior?

What I am appealing to in all of this is common sense. You can argue for "full restoration" and miss this obvious fact. The lack of blamelessness in his life carries with it severe and lasting reproach. Can his wife ever forget what he did to her? Will his children always know that their dad was unfaithful to their mother—an adulterer? And will his flock know that he violated the sanctity of holy marriage as well as his ordination vows? All of the forgiveness given by each of the above will not remove the reproach he has taken to himself for the rest of his life.

A RIGHT ATTITUDE NEEDED

Because of the pastor's position, the consequences of his actions cannot be ignored. Yet we also cannot ignore the need for forgiveness and the possibility of some form of restoration. With that qualification in mind, how do we proceed with the process of restoration? First, each of us must aproach the fallen leader with humility. We must be fully aware of our own sinfulness. Surely none who considers this pressing issue should do so with any degree of self-righteousness regarding his own standing. He must always "take heed lest he too fall."

CHURCHES HAVE OFTEN TREATED FALLEN PASTORS AS VIRTUAL LEPERS, TO BE DISCARDED AND REJECTED WHEN EXPOSED. [THIS] SPEAKS TRAGICALLY OF THE COUNTER-BIBLICAL ATTITUDES OF OUR DAY.

"Righteous and a Sinner"

Martin Luther coined a phrase for the proper attitude we should have regarding ourselves when we come to any subject that deals with the sins of others. Here we find a correct understanding of ourselves before God and the gospel: *simul justus et peccator* (literally, "at the same time righteous and a sinner"). This phrase perfectly combines what Luther knew himself to be—righteous, fully and perfectly, but simultaneously, a sinner.

Perfectionistic thinking about the Christian life is both unbiblical and unhealthy. Inevitably perfectionism sets believers up for a serious fall, precisely because they do not come to grips with their remaining corruption and the indwelling power of sin. Even the most faithful pastor must see and feel the impact of the well-known truth: "There but for the grace of God go I."

This is not the place for hubris, ministerial condescension, or unbiblical lovelessness. In dealing with such a sensitive area as the life of a fallen pastor, his family and his ministry, nothing could be more needed in terms of personal attitude and response than mercy. Self-righteous judgment must be earnestly resisted. We must grow up into a kind of ministry that "speaks the truth in love." Only with tears will we be properly able to open up this subject. The fact that churches have often treated fallen pastors as virtual lepers, to be discarded and rejected when exposed, speaks tragically of the counter-biblical attitudes of our day.

A friend wrote of churches being "quick with the hammer and slow with the hand." I am afraid he is right. Churches very infrequently exercise proper discipline in our time. Generally they ignore discipline until a pastor sins publicly. Then they come down with swift and harsh judgment. The offender feels no hope for the future. This often "provokes to anger" in much the same way parental discipline does when it is improperly administered (Ephesians 6:3).

The fallen pastor can be forgiven, and he can become an effective servant of God again. How spiritual leaders and the congregation respond can make a significant difference in the spiritual healing of this broken man. Having seen churches respond to tragedies over the years I am convinced that only some undertake the restoration of a fallen pastor with good understanding.

Advice from Galatians

The counsel of Galatians 6:1 needs to be considered more carefully if a right attitude and approach is to be taken. Here, Paul writes: "Brethren, even if a man is caught in any trespass, you who are spiritual, restore such a one in a spirit of gentleness, each one looking to yourself, lest you too be tempted."

How are we to restore one fallen in sin? "In a spiritual manner, and gently," Paul answers. "And let's always look to ourselves, because we too can be tempted and fall."

The apostle uses the word *katartizo* to describe the final goal of restoration. *Katartizo* means to mend or repair. It is a word that was used literally for setting a broken bone or putting a dislocated limb back into place. Hendriksen suggests that the main idea is: "Follow a positive, not a negative, course with respect to the trespasser. Do not hurt him but help him. Treat him as you yourselves would wish to be treated if you were in his place."[1] I suggest that all who enter into this difficult problem, especially pastors and deacons, need to seek the complete recovery of the fallen pastor. The fallen pastor's forgiveness before God must be acknowledged and properly supported when he humbly asks for it. His repentance must be accepted, with hopefulness, as long as his lifestyle is consistent with his public and private confession. Only when you have wept with the broken pastor who has shattered his life through such sin can you appreciate the depth of feeling and pain that goes with the process of ongoing repentance and spiritual restoration.

Having said that, let's remember that the sole issue is not recovery to ministry, as our therapeutically oriented age is inclined to believe. We should desire the minister's full repentance and his walking once again in practical holiness before God. That is both the beginning and end of the whole process, and that goal must be sought. But there is much more to be considered in the scenario of a fallen pastor. If you love the church you must be concerned about what has happened to the church. How will the church deal with the reproach brought upon the people and their corporate witness? Further, what does biblical fidelity truly require of us in such situations?

GRACE AND FORGIVENESS

First, the pastor and congregation alike need a proper understanding of the meaning of grace and forgiveness. Yes, our heavenly Father offers total forgiveness, and His grace means we do nothing to earn His favor.

Yet when someone says, "God 'casts our sin as far as the east is from the west' (Psalm 103:12) and so must we," we cannot ignore the impact of the sin. Forgetting the past is not what the psalmist has in view here, especially in God's forgiveness, for how can an omniscient Being forget anything? What is meant in this expression is this: God will never hold to the account of a repentant sinner what He has forgiven. It is as good as forgotten. Why? Because we will never hear of it from Him again. We will not be chargeable for it in any sense. It is an impossibility that he shall be asked to atone for it, or pay for it in any fashion. This is why the text says, "I will remember them against you no more."

Remembering the Sin

Fallen pastors, along with Christians in general, need to be urged to stop calling people's remembrance of past scandal a "lack of forgiveness." Forgiveness means we can forgive one who has wronged us, if they confess their sin and ask my forgiveness. It also means choosing, by God's grace, to never bring up this person's sin to the individual or to others. Furthermore, we can choose not to nurse our own feelings of hurt and bitterness when they arise. Indeed, we must forgive in this manner, or we can question whether we are children of God, led by His Spirit (cf. Matthew 6:12–15; 18:21, 35; Mark 11:26; Ephesians 4:32; Colossians 3:13). We can show heartfelt forgiveness, yet our fallen leaders must recognize that their choices— every choice we all make—have inherent consequences that last throughout this lifetime.

The church has historically dealt more kindly with converted sinners who previously lived in reckless moral abandon than with members who later backslide into sinful living. We observed this pattern particularly in the early church. The contemporary believer should be no different. A Christian professes allegiance to Christ, unites with the church, and leaves the world system behind. He follows the Savior and is different. He is called to be holy and separate from the world and its corruption. The believer has "tasted" the grace of God. He has come into the light if he is truly one of Christ's own. What if he turns back to the world and embraces what he knows and understands to be morally bankrupt? There are spiritual and personal consequences.

A Pastor's Impact

When the one turning back to the world is a pastor, there can be little doubt that the consequences will be grave. We are not concerned, to put it simply, with the ordinary member of a local church. As Calvin wrote, "This is the artifice of Satan—to seek some misconduct on the part of ministers, that they may tend to the dishonor of the gospel."[2]

With the pastor we are concerned with one whose reputation is everything if he would succeed in a genuinely spiritual ministry. Elton Trueblood wrote of this factor some years ago when he said,

> It is hard to think of any job in which the moral element is lacking. The skill of the dentist is wholly irrelevant if he is unprincipled and irresponsible. There is little in that case to keep him from withdrawing teeth unnecessarily, because the patient is usually in a helpless situation. It is easy to see the harm that can be done by an unprincipled lawyer. Indeed such a man is far more dangerous if he is skilled than if he is not skilled.[3]

After quoting Trueblood, Charles Swindoll added,

> You and I [i.e., pastors] are dangerous people, because we are skilled people. We have influence, we make an impact in a community. . . . I've never been asked to show my GPA in ministry. Nobody's ever asked about the grades I made in school. But I have been checked again and again and again and again in character, because the ministry is a character profession.[4]

This is precisely why some pastors reveal their own deception so completely when they insist that they stopped short of the actual physical act, and only engaged in an "impropriety" or "improper sexual behavior." Sometimes a man will refrain from certain actions according to a rigid set of cleverly defined moral principles, yet at the same time his life is completely dominated by the very sin he thinks he has not yet committed.

Remember, non-Christians can and sometimes do live by good moral standards, even standards that approximate the norms of biblical behavior to a large extent. What is called for in the Christian, and especially in the gospel minister, is consistent living by the gospel which empowers him to "love his wife as Christ loved the church." Only this will sustain both his life and his doctrine before both God and the visible church. Only this will preserve him from the sexual impurity that breaks this divine model.

RESTORE TO FELLOWSHIP WITH GOD
Repentance

Second, after a proper understanding of forgiveness, the sexually fallen pastor needs to be restored to God. He has recognized his sinfulness and seeks forgiveness from the God he has offended. He now repents.

[THE PASTOR] MUST RUN TO CHRIST FOR CLEANSING . . . . WHAT HE IS SEEKING IS "A BROKEN AND CONTRITE HEART." HE DOES NOT DARE TO TRUST HIMSELF. HE TRUSTS ONLY THE GOSPEL.

Though the consequences of his sin may end his marriage, destroy his family, and surely must end his present pastoral labors, restoration with God is possible. This is the first and most important issue a pastor will face when his sin has been brought home to him by the Spirit. He must labor with all that is in him to "work out his own salvation with fear and trembling" (Philippians 2:12).

When a pastor falls into the arms of another woman his fall is great. His sin threatens his own soul more than he knows. Apostasy is a very real danger (1 Corinthians 9:27), and his past profession is seriously called into question at this time. He may very well be a backslidden Christian, but if he seeks falsely to comfort himself by this observation he may do untold harm to his own soul.

What he feels, if he is "brought to his senses" (Luke 15·17), is his own helpless estate. He cannot read his salvation clearly, even if he has been a regenerate man for many years. He feels condemned, sometimes hopeless and completely hypocritical. And for good reason, for unless he repents, which itself is a gift of God, he will have no future assurance of relationship with God. What he knows at this moment of deep conviction is that he has sinned, and he cannot believe the complete mess he has made of his life. He knows he has grieved the Holy Spirit and that he has lived treacherously. He knows that he must run to Christ for cleansing or he will not be clean (Psalm 51). What he is seeking is "a broken and contrite heart." He does not dare to trust himself. He trusts only the gospel, which alone can cause him to stand again.

A Sense of Grief

It is desirable that a fallen minister feels the weight of his sin, the heinousness of what he has done in his sexual infidelity, and the need for full and complete repentance before God. This is what David was doing in Psalm 51. The reason God gave us this Psalm is not that we might tearfully use it in a public manner in order to be restored to ministry promptly. It is a private lamentation of deep feeling made public and given to the church "as an example . . . for our instruction" (1 Corinthians 10:11).

Repentance is more than the response of a moment. It is much more than feelings of shame and guilt, which may overwhelm us for a season. It is an evangelical saving grace, whereby a sinner, with a true sense of his sin, and an apprehension of the mercy of God in Christ, with grief and hatred of his sin, turns from sin to God. It includes a full, whole-hearted endeavor to obey God, especially in the areas where the failure has occurred.[5]

Sorrow and Change

One vital element of true repentance, often missing in our psychotherapeutic age, is the loathing of self that brings lasting and complete change. Ezekiel tells us that the Spirit's work, through the gospel itself, will cause the following response: "Then you will remember your evil ways and your deeds that were not good, and you will loathe yourselves in your own sight for your iniquities and your abominations" (Ezekiel 36:31). Such repentance causes one to be "pierced to the heart" (Acts 2:37) and "produces a repentance without regret, leading to salvation . . . for behold what earnestness this very thing, this godly sorrow, has produced in you" (2 Corinthians 7:10–11).

IN AN AGE OF MICROWAVE SPIRITUALITY, HE MUST NOT HURRY THIS PROCESS. TIME ALONE WILL NOT HEAL ALL THINGS.

A fallen brother, who has privately shared with me many of his own personal thoughts, once wrote me:

> While every instance of moral failure is different, there is one constant: there must be "fruits of repentance" that God produces and the sinner and the body of Christ recognize. Only God can produce those fruits that are acceptable to Him and affirming to the fallen man himself. It is when God is pleased to mercifully permit opportunities of ministry that one begins to sense the validation of acceptable fruits of repentance. Thus, to initiate opportunities through some man-created process defined by time, weakens the affirmation process of God-produced restoration. There can be no greater validation of healing and restoration than the father sovereignly granting ministry opportunities solely apart from the initiation of man. The timing of such validation must be left in God's hands, not instituted by man. Only then can the joy of "repentance without regret" be experienced (2 Cor. 7:10). When this occurs, motivation for ministry becomes based upon gratitude and not desire for public success.

Before considering any future ministry—why or why not, where or when—the fallen pastor needs to be encouraged in a new pursuit of God through true repentance. He must be crushed by his sin, and this will bring him near despair. Quick healing is never desirable, lest the wound not be cleansed by God through the Word (cf. 2 Corinthians 2:5–11).

If his confession and repentance are real, he will not seek primarily to keep his office. His desire, motivated by brokenness, will be to protect God's people and to preserve them. The effects of his failure upon God's Name and God's people will become his chief concerns.

In an age of microwave spirituality, he must not hurry this process. Time alone will not heal all things. It might make them worse, adding deception to more deception. Unless the fallen pastor recognizes the dangers of his own deception I fear he can never escape the trap his sin has woven and the consequences which will likely bring him down again.

A. W. Tozer, himself a pastor who spoke often regarding the matter of true repentance and its relationship to Christian experience, has explained what is involved:

> One vital test of all religious experience is how it affects our relation to God, our concept of God and our attitude toward Him. Any doctrine, any experience that serves to magnify Him is likely to be inspired by Him.
>
> The heart of man is like a musical instrument and may be played upon by the Holy Spirit, by an evil spirit or by the spirit of man himself. Religious emotions are very much the same, no matter who the player may be. . . .
>
> The big test is, What has this done to my relationship to the God and father of our Lord Jesus Christ (Rev. 4:11)? . . . The true nature of the phenomenon (i.e., the spiritual experience) is discovered later when the face of Christ begins to fade from the victim's consciousness.
>
> If on the other hand the new experience tends to make Christ indispensable, if it takes our interest off our feelings and places it in Christ, we are on the right track. Whatever makes Christ dear to us is pretty sure to be from God (Matt. 3:17; Acts 2:36; 4:12; John 14:6).
>
> It may be stated unequivocally that any spirit that permits compromise with the world is a false spirit. . . . The operations of grace within the heart of a believing man will turn that heart away from sin and toward holiness. . . . I do not see how it could be plainer. The same grace that saves teaches that saved man inwardly, and its teaching is

both negative and positive. Negatively it teaches us to deny ungodliness and worldly lusts. Positively it teaches us to live soberly, righteously and godly, right in this present world.

The man of honest heart will find no difficulty here. He has but to check his own bent to discover whether he is concerned about sin in his life more or less since the supposed work of grace was done.[6]

Because sin destroys inward graces, weakens personal resolve, and corrupts the believer's hope, the fallen pastor must not take his own repentance lightly. His whole life depends on how thoroughly he seeks God for a repentant heart that is true and full. Here is where any consideration of restoration must always begin.

It is troubling that most of the literature on this subject, and that from evangelical sources, addresses the psychological aspects of the fallen pastor's sexual sin: Why did I do this? What needs have been unmet in my life? What happened to me so that I was set up for my fall? How can I gain better understanding regarding my repressed feelings? Few of these approaches seem to come to grips with what Tozer is saying in the above statements. Almost all take repentance to be something that is easy so long as you "feel sorrow" for what you did. Godly sorrow is much more difficult.

RESTORE TO THE FAMILY

Third, the pastor needs to be restored to his family. At the moment the fallen pastor's sin is discovered, either through his own admission, or by uncovering the situation through other means, the process of seeking to restore the man to God, his family, and the church begins.

Because the sexually fallen pastor has sinned against his wife and his children, he must seek the forgiveness of those hurt the most deeply by his sin. He must earnestly desire reconciliation with those touched by the knowledge of his sin. If he is to experience any meaningful restoration, as much as is possible, this step must be taken.

The Wife's Response

What complicates this part of the process is this—his wife may forgive him upon his confession, but she may choose not to be reconciled to him as a marriage partner, and with good reason. He has violated the covenant of marriage and destroyed their sacred bond (Matthew 5:31–32; 19:3–9). She may choose to forgive him, but she does not choose to remain married to him. His sin has, in the way referred to by Jesus Himself, broken the marriage.

It is interesting to note that for this reason many Protestant Reformers, in distinction from Roman Catholic moralists, believed that adultery ended the original marriage. Only when the sinful party sought reconciliation and the offended party agreed to a new marriage was the covenant again established between this particular man and this particular woman.

The sinning pastor must understand. He has killed his own marriage. If his wife responds by glossing over her husband's sin too easily, as is sometimes the case, she may add to his deception regarding both the patterns that led him into this sin and the damage that he has caused. If she remains with her husband but does not seek to build a new relationship, using the old problems to attack him, then this too will bring untold harm.

The much overused concept of victimization is destroying personal responsibility in our culture. However, it is a profound truth that the most severely affected victim in pastoral adultery is the man's wife. It is almost criminal to observe how often members of the church blame the wife for her husband's sin. The old canard that "There is no innocent party," and "There are always two sides to an affair in a marriage" might have elements of truth, but the Scripture enjoins us to offer solid support and help to the person who is the victim.

The Pastor's Duty to His Family

The fallen pastor needs to confess his sin to his wife and his children, if they are of the age where it is appropriate. He needs humbly to ask for their forgiveness and to be willing to wait, not demanding anything from them, as it is he who has destroyed their trust in him as a person.

The church leadership can help the pastor in this area. Elders or members of an executive committee might tell the pastor of his duty in seeking reconciliation with his family, or at least inquire as to whether he has properly approached the family yet. They might offer him a short leave to permit him to take care of family matters; perhaps this should even be required as part of an extended time away from church duties.)

RESTORE TO THE CHURCH

When it is appropriate, the fallen pastor needs to confess to his extended church family. This is the fourth step in reconciliation. The pastor should be advised to be careful in how he does this. He does not need to name the events, persons, places, etc. He does need to humbly admit that he has sinned so grievously that he must give up his office as pastor, being disqualified from holding it by virtue of what he has done.

When the pastor fails to admit his sin in the face of solid evidence and proper investigation, which we will consider in the next chapter, he must be treated as the sinning brother in 1 Corinthians 5. His lack of cooperation with the process of restoration through honest confession and repentance conveys the deepest sort of pride and personal deception. Until he will acknowledge his sin before the Lord, his family and his church (as appropriate), no process of public restoration can even begin. If necessary, he must be removed from the church or presbytery, as the case may be, by an act of discipline.

Since many surveys reveal that 65 percent or more of those pastors who sexually fall do so with someone in the church body, this means he should also seek the forgiveness of the woman (or women) involved in his sin directly. This too must be handled with discretion, for every situation will be different. A simple statement asking for forgiveness is probably all that is in order, given the danger of further contact with the person he has been involved with. He may even need to seek out the husband of one or more women, though this is even more problematic, given the fact that many more lives are now at stake in the knowledge of the offense (see Proverbs 6:32–35). As a rule he should make the knowledge of his offense only as wide as is absolutely necessary, and always sparing the specific details (Ephesians 5:11–12).

PUBLIC CONFESSION

What if the sin becomes public knowledge? Clearly a public rebuke is in order in light of lesser sins confessed before "all." If lesser sins are confessed openly, then in some form public confession is also necessary for the sexually fallen pastor. A detailed confession is not enjoined by the text for sure, but it is a confession no less. Some argue that such "invades the right of privacy" that the pastor has. I reason differently—leaders have forfeited the so-called "right to privacy" when they accept the church's call to serve as a pastor. Their entire life has a public quality about it. They are to be models of godliness for the church. The public does have the right to know if the pastor's life is what he preaches and professes.

Public rebuke seems to be the norm in Scripture, while today we continue to move further from this approach, either because of fear or ignorance. Lawsuits threaten us when we seek to carry out proper church discipline. Even bodily harm has been threatened against pastors who become involved in corrective discipline. In spite of these factors, we observe that Paul rebuked Peter and Barnabas publicly (Galatians 2:11–14). And consider Nathan's approach to David (2 Samuel 12). This may have been private in his first approach, but God made it public in order that we might learn by it.

It seems, to put it simply, that God isn't concerned about the reputations of immoral pastors being exposed. It is often because of a rather unusual providence that God exposes such sin, when it has been hidden for months or years. God is far more concerned with His own holiness and with the purity of His church being preserved than with the cover-up of a pastor's scandalous behavior.

The point of Paul's exhortation to Timothy in 5:19–20 is twofold. First, he wanted to protect elders from false and slanderous accusations that might wrongly bring down their ministry. When adultery is the charge, and the pastor does not admit it, an investigation must proceed with caution, but it must proceed. Various church traditions and denominations have devised fair and effective ways for doing this. Where they exist they should be utilized consistently, and where they do not exist churches should consider establishing guidelines for how they will handle the instruction of this text in a practical manner.

Second, Paul's exhortation was meant to show that elders who sin do so with no more impunity than others. In fact, they must be disciplined even more severely than others. The law made this same distinction (see Leviticus 4:22, 27).

How should such a confession take place? In most cases the fallen pastor should be urged to confess the failure before the church family at the close of a public service, probably in a meeting held after a morning church service. The meeting can be led by either a respected leader from within the local church or an outside leader known to the church. When this is done, an announcement can be made at the close of the service, inviting non-members to leave as "the church family has an important matter to concern itself with which is extremely sensitive."

The fallen pastor can read a prepared statement indicating his repentance and regret. Afterward, the leader/moderator should urge a season of prayer. Finally, the pastor (and perhaps his wife and family) should remain where people can speak with him, offering proper, prayerful encouragement.

The moderator should explain to the members the procedure that will be followed in the ensuing months as the pastor seeks to put his life back together and serve his family. The moderator should be very clear that the pastor's ministry is over, lest sympathetic members begin to promote his return to office. Reports of progress in emotional and spiritual recovery should be given to the church in the months that follow as the restoration committee begins its work of helping restore the fallen man to complete spiritual health.

AN IMPORTANT CAUTION

Because many have fallen, the assumption often is that a pastor who is charged with sexual impropriety is guilty. A strong caution is in order. Congregationally governed churches are particularly open to mishandling such charges, as they often do not have a clear process for hearing the charges in private. They often do not process the charges properly, coming to a conclusion that is both accurate and helpful.

Paul's counsel to Timothy is needed in an age where so many have fallen and accusations of all kinds fly here and there. If we would handle these matters properly we must study and obey his counsel with utmost care: "Do not receive an accusation against an elder except on the basis of two or three witnesses. Those who continue in sin, rebuke in the presence of all, so that the rest also may be fearful of sinning" (1 Timothy 5:19–20).

> *SPECIAL TREATMENT, WHICH PUTS THE PASTOR ABOVE THE REST OF THE FLOCK, IS CLEARLY NOT THE POINT. FAIR TREATMENT AND PROTECTION FROM CAPRICIOUS ACCUSATIONS ARE WHAT IS IN VIEW.*

In 1 Timothy 5:17–20, Paul is plainly instructing the church in the matter of recognizing and disciplining pastors. In the verses quoted above he warns against accepting an accusation against an elder (pastor) unless two or three witnesses support the charge. Special treatment, which puts the pastor above the rest of the flock, is clearly not the point. Fair treatment and protection from capricious accusations are what is in view. Lea and Griffin note in *The New American Commentary,* "The church leader should enjoy at least as much protection as the ordinary Jew had under the law (see Deuteronomy 17:6; 19:15)."[7]

Paul's counsel in verse 20 raises three questions. First, who was involved in the sinning? The answer of the context is clearly "elders." The tense for sinning here is present, meaning that the practice was continuous and not merely one isolated occurrence. Second, before whom was this rebuke to take place? It could be their fellow elders or even the church body itself. The phrase "in the presence of all" seems to suggest a larger group; thus some believe the entire congregation is in view. Perhaps the elders would examine the case and give report to the whole church.

The third question is this: who are the "rest" who are to be "fearful of sinning" because this knowledge is made known to them? Some say the entire church, while still others refer this to the remaining elders who are aware of the case. I believe Paul wanted the whole congregation to fear God in this scenario, lest they fall also. As is written in *The New American Commentary*, "Paul did not envision a vendetta, but he wanted to avoid partiality toward important leaders and provide fair treatment for all."[8]

Did the sins spoken of include adultery? Lenski thinks not, noting that "such cases are to be brought before the congregation itself, which gave the office and which alone can again take it away." However, he adds, the participle does not "refer to the gravest kind of sinning 'like fornication, drunkenness, and the like.'" Thus in those situations, "That such elders should be allowed to retain their office is rather incredible."[9]

CONCLUSION

Remember, the goal in the restoration process is that we gently assist in the recovery of sexually fallen pastors, remembering our own temptations to fall. Instead of being self-righteous and arrogant, rude and evasive, let us do what Paul goes on to say in Galatians 6:2, and "bear one another's burdens, and thus fulfill the law of Christ." In this loving act, we will be fulfilling Christ's commandment that we "love one another, even as [He] has loved [us]" (John 13:34).

When the damage of sexual misconduct threatens to destroy the church, the time is right for leaders to display humility, repentance, and a specific seeking of the face of God for both the fallen man and the life of the local church.

NOTES

1. William Hendriksen, *New Testament Commentary: Galatians* (Grand Rapids, Mich.: Baker, 1968), 231–32.

2. Graham Miller, Comp.; *Calvin's Wisdom* (Carlisle, Pa.: Banner of Truth, 1992), 217.

3. As Quoted in Charles Swindoll, "The Integrity of the Spiritual Leader" from a message given at the Christian Booksellers Convention, 1987, and excerpted in *Grace Today,* October 1987, 1.

4. Ibid, 10.

5. *Westminster Shorter Catechism,* Question 87.

6. A. W. Tozer, *Man: The Dwelling Place of God* (Harrisburg, Pa.: Christian Publications, 1966), 119–133.

7. Thomas D. Lea and Hayne P. Griffin, Jr., *The New American Commentary: 1, 2 Timothy and Titus* (Nashville, Tenn.: Broadman, 1992), 156.

8. Ibid., 157.

9. R. C. H. Lenski, *The Interpretation of St. Paul's Epistles to the Colossians, to the Thessalonians, to Timothy, to Titus and to Philemon* (Minneapolis, Minn.: Augsburg, 1937), 685.

CHAPTER ELEVEN

GUARDING AGAINST MISCONDUCT

The Christian ministry is the worst of all trades, but the best of all professions.

John Newton

As I have listened to the sad confessions of sexually fallen pastors I have often said to myself, "If only he had taken steps to avoid this fall in the first place!" Pastors clearly bear the primary responsibility for avoiding the sexual temptation that leads to moral failure. But the church also needs to better understand what is happening in our present environment.

Simply put, both church and pastor need to take clear and decisive action to avoid even the appearance of sexual impropriety. And churches need to increasingly adopt steps that will safeguard their shepherds from becoming casualties to the moral quicksand of our sexually explicit age.

In this chapter we will consider some of the practical ways in which both the church and the pastor can take preventive steps regarding sexual misconduct.

THE CHURCH'S CONTRIBUTION

The local church, as well as denominational bodies, need to understand the magnitude of this problem if they are to take seriously the role they can have in preventing it. Sexual temptations are so much a part of our present cultural scene that we have tended toward being desensitized regarding them.

Regardless of the governmental structure adopted by a local church, the leaders (elders, deacons, church council, etc.) must become involved in fresh commitment to radical purity. In your church that may be a board of elders or it may be a church council or executive committee. Increasingly, churches are floundering and self-destructing as a result of the moral tragedies that often go unknown to the general public.

Churches must take fuller responsibility for ordaining and placing men in the ministry. Men with prior emotional and sexual problems should not be ordained, unless their offense is so far removed from their present lifestyle that it is not even a minor question. Investigation into these matters must be honest and careful. Like marriage, it is better to wait and be sure, than to plunge ahead and have to deal with major problems after the fact.

In this same vein seminaries could help the local church by more personal involvement in the character development of those students who aspire to pastoral ministry. The typical internship requirements do not suffice in the training and checking that need to go on before a man becomes a pastor. If a degree program is designed to actually prepare men for pastoral leadership, then a minimum requirement for his education ought to be the development of character. The proper use of the Christian disciplines should be a requirement for divinity students.

But what can the leadership of the local church actually do about the problem of sexual misconduct in the life of the pastor? Isn't this really a problem that is to be left entirely to the personal discretion of the pastor himself?

1. Understand the Nature of Pastoral Leadership

Let me answer this question first by observing that the pastor may not desire the involvement of faithful lay leadership. When a pastor does not want the support and involvement of lay leaders, he is already in grave danger. He has clearly forgotten his role—that of a servant leader.

Integrity must be seen and continually proven if a man is to function well in pastoral ministry. Time and again the sexual fall of a minister is the direct result of an abuse of his office and the power associated with it. The sexual sin becomes, in other words, the revelation of an even deeper problem—the failure of basic integrity in vital areas of leadership.

Hudson T. Armerding, former president of Wheaton College and a student of leadership principles, has written:

> Some important qualifications that should characterize Christian leadership are set forth in Acts 6:3. The early church was instructed by the Holy Spirit through the apostles to seek out those who had a good reputation, a demonstrated wisdom and the fullness of the Holy Spirit. In other words, these leaders were to have moral integrity, intellectual competence and spiritual vitality.[1]

If a pastor is to lead the church, he must keep proving his character and displaying genuine servant leadership over a long period of time. Otherwise his integrity will break down and his leadership will ultimately fail, if not sooner, then later.

As leaders in churches, we need to better understand the biblical nature of leadership. The false expectations we have placed upon the work of pastoral ministry actually set up many of our brothers for the serious falls that have occurred. Compare, for instance, the leadership patterns in churches in the West with those in China. The findings of veteran church observer David Wang in *Evangelicals Now*, a monthly evangelical paper published in Great Britain, indirectly suggest ways that American churches might limit the amount of sexual sin in the pastorate.

In the West leadership is formal and comes from authority above. It is generally based on "capability" in society and charisma, dress, style, and manner. It usually develops out of diplomas, certificates, and organizational skills. In China leadership is much more informal. Endorsement of leadership comes from "below" as people see character develop and lifestyle proven over time. It is much more a matter of spiritual giftedness and this in a way that does not promote the "superstar" approach. Leadership follows a period of true testing, which is much more thorough than training in a school, and is organism centered, rather than market-driven and management-directed. Prayer is central to leadership in China, while in the West we tend to talk about spiritual things more than actually do them. In our culture leaders are rewarded based on performance, a tricky thing to say the least, while in China leaders face persecution, along with the loss of family. These stress points make the desire for leadership quite different than what we know in most Western churches. Our churches are results oriented, while in China the measurement tends to be "potential under God." Here, leadership is often viewed, whether spoken or unspoken, as a climb up a ladder, while in China there is no ladder, unless it is one which brings greater opportunity for suffering.

Finally, we major on "high profile" and being "in charge," while in China high profile is viewed as detrimental to being a true servant of people.[2]

Can we escape these Western cultural patterns? Not fully. But we must aim higher. We must war against the sinful directions of our culture that influence the church so powerfully. And we must avoid echoing the celebrity mentality and "meet my need" cries of our society in our churches. Otherwise we shall continue to attract pastors who use and abuse, displaying that they are not following the patterns of servant leadership.

Remember, authority in the New Testament was never autocratic but rather derived. It was under Christ and exercised through a servant attitude. I fear we have missed this by such a wide measure that until churches define their understanding of these things much more biblically we have no hope of escaping the traps we create for potential failure.

The pastor must be a spiritual leader before he is a decision maker. He must be much more than a charismatic figure who develops and leads a dynamic organization of people. His walk with God must be of first importance and the church must understand and encourage this. It seems that the typical church board often has little understanding of these dimensions and their importance. Part of the blame for the failure of pastors can be attributable to this.

2. Provide an Umbrella of Understanding

The church, furthermore, can supply a kind of umbrella of protection, especially in the area of sexual temptation. It is wise that the church approach this discreetly, not violating the personal life of the pastor.

The church can supply this umbrella by understanding some of the basic demands that are placed upon the pastor. The minister finds himself under constant pressure and acute temptation. He must prepare his sermons, counsel those in need, guide and administer the affairs of the church body, attend functions of many kinds, visit the sick, comfort the sorrowing, seek to find and reach the lost, care for his wife and family, and preserve his own health. In addition, he must take care of his own soul, feeding himself and watching his life with diligence. In some ways it is truly amazing more pastors do not fail, which in itself is a tribute to the grace of God.

Tim LaHaye, formerly pastor of a large southern California church, understands all of this well when he writes: "Perhaps no profession is so geared to making its leader a working machine. But no matter how diligent the effort, the result is never quite satisfactory. Most ministers rarely go home with the satisfaction of knowing that all tasks have been completed."[3]

LaHaye calls for churches to insist more directly that men take time off for true rest. Several churches have recently begun to use the concept of a "sabbatical" as well. The lay leadership should seek whatever program the church can afford and properly support in an effort to help protect the pastor from a sexual fall.

In addition, lay leaders need to get closer to the pressures and demands of the pastoral ministry. Nothing hurts more deeply than to hear the continual joke about pastors "working only one day a week." If this foolishness is believed by the church then they surely share in some of the blame for their pastor's moral failure when it happens.

3. Recognize a Leader's Seasons of Danger

The danger the leader faces with an overbearing workload was first obvious in the story of Jethro advising Moses (see Exodus 18:18, 21–22). As a leader, Moses felt his presence was needed for every decision, both great and small. In Jethro's wise plan of delegating, Moses was delivered from complete breakdown. May God give to every pastor at least one Jethro who can watch for stress points and help him in this manner.

WE NEED TO ENCOURAGE THE PASTOR, NOT FLATTER HIM. REMEMBERING MINISTRY ANNIVERSARIES, BIRTHDAYS, AND SPECIAL ACCOMPLISHMENTS ALL TEND TO STRENGTHEN THE WEARY SHEPHERD'S RESOLVE TO REMAIN FAITHFUL TO THE WORK.

Most of us are aware that there are times in our lives when we are under particular stress. At these times our resistance might be low. Our spirits are overtaxed and our bodies are weary. Jay Kesler has suggested that pastors are particularly susceptible to temptation after failing to achieve all that they had planned or hoped. Or that men are inclined to yield to various temptations when they have completed a major task. He adds that as men enter their middle years, when they seek to determine the value of their lives, they can be more vulnerable. Church leadership that would truly support their pastor and seek to prevent failure must understand that these seasons are times of special danger for every man.[4]

We must remember, at this point, the great success of the prophet Elijah in 1 Kings 18. No doubt he was thrilled when he saw God send fire out of heaven in answer to his cry. The success he enjoyed was unparalleled. Yet in the next chapter he is defeated in his spirit and begging God to end his life. Similarly, at different seasons of life, and at different points in ministry, a pastor is prone to temptation, disappointment, and sin. We must be alert to that and support our pastors.

Faithful members of the flock, and leaders in particular, must observe the seasons of their pastor's ministry. We need to encourage the pastor, not flatter him. Remembering ministry anniversaries, birthdays, and special accomplishments all tend to strengthen the weary shepherd's resolve to remain faithful to the work of the particular church he serves. Much of what passes for praise is flattery at the back door, nor true encouragement that reflects deep appreciation and support. Every leader needs at least one Barnabas and every pastor needs several fellow leaders who will watch out for his life in a proper way.

4. Anticipate the Potential Legal Problems

Church leaders must understand that courts and public agencies are increasingly holding the local church responsible for pastoral indiscretion in the areas of sexual or financial abuse. Brent Walker, general counsel for the Washington-based Baptist Joint Committee, has said, "More clergy are sued for sexual misconduct than for any other reason. . . . It is much wiser and easier, not to mention more cost effective, for churches to take steps to avoid this problem than to deal with its consequences." And in the same 1994 report Walker said, "Most importantly, churches should do this for the sake of preventing harm to potential victims." Concerning church liability, Walker noted, "Courts are increasingly extending liability to the church or organization where they (i.e., the sexually abusive leader) work."[5]

Walker suggested several precautions churches should take regarding this problem. I give only a sample of them:

1. Conduct a thorough background check when hiring ministers and other employees and soliciting volunteers, paying particular attention to any allegations of sexual misconduct.

2. A minister, or other church employee, should normally be suspended from work while any investigation is ongoing into such potential sexual misconduct. The church has an obligation to protect those charged until a full and fair investigation has taken place. This should be done as privately as possible.

3. Churches have a moral and legal obligation to disclose substantiated incidents of sexual misconduct when a prospective employer inquires about a former minister's employment record.[6]

One 350-member congregation in Florida, after having had three pastoral ministries devastated due to sexual misconduct, was almost destroyed. The current pastor told his denominational paper how the church investigated his background by actually hiring a private detective. In addition, the church search committee wanted members of the candidate's present church involved in the process before he left for the new church. Many questions were asked to determine the state of his own marriage as well.[7] A moment's reflection will cause the reader to see why this church took such strong measures to assure itself that it would not be destroyed by another scandal.

Protection and Prevention

Clearly churches need to be involved in protection and prevention when it comes to potential sexual failure of their pastors. And in all this, balance is needed to protect the pastor and the local church.

The church must preserve a delicate balance when seeking to help the pastor withstand immorality. To sacrifice his leadership because some have failed would be a travesty of the worst kind. However, to refuse to support him with all of the resources needed is an equal, if not greater

evil. The moral climate of this day and the pressures of the ministry
can combine to wreak havoc in a minister's personal life. The care a
pastor requires ought to be the highest priority of those who gain the
most from his labor.[8]

THE PASTOR'S ROLE IN PREVENTION

If a pastor desires to avoid sexual sin, he must take active
personal responsibility for his life and decisions. In our present
climate he is in grave danger already if he concludes, falsely,
that he can't help himself. This type of fatalistic thinking can
lead him to believe that he feels and acts as he does because of
what others have done to him. He must know that God holds
him fully responsible for all his actions. No reasons can explain
away his sinful choices for which God and the church must
hold him fully accountable.

To avoid succumbing to the temptation of adultery, the
pastor must develop a thorough-going, comprehensive plan for
protecting himself. Here are several elements that you as a pastor could consider in developing such a plan for prevention.

1. Understand the Nature of Sexual Temptation

Sexual feelings are common to every man and woman.
Sometimes these feelings are neither understood nor accepted
in a truly healthy way. This is particularly true when Christians, in particular, may regard their sexual feelings in a strictly negative way. But God made us sexual beings, and our
sexuality is healthy, and much more than the physical set of
actions that constitute union between a man and a woman.
The sexual union is simply a physical expression of the emotional and spiritual bond formed between two people.

Sexual feelings, of course, must be guarded to find proper
expression. For any person, including the pastor, to avoid sexual feelings that lead to sinful expression, *he must seek wisdom*.
This trait is like having a lifeguard always on duty. Finding
wisdom is the theme of Proverbs; here we find the truth, "For
wisdom will enter your heart, and knowledge will be pleasant
to your soul; discretion will guard you, understanding will
watch over you" (2:10–11, cf. 16).

A pastor who shows wisdom regarding his sexuality knows that he could enter into a relationship with a woman that is quite sexual without ever touching her or entering into an obviously illicit relationship. As Pastor Randy Alcorn wrote, "Just because I'm not touching a woman, or just because I'm not envisioning specific erotic encounters, does not mean I'm not becoming sexually involved with her."[9]

THE MINISTER MUST ANTICIPATE AND PREVENT SEXUAL TEMPTATIONS. ANONYMITY AND LEISURE TIME SPELL CATASTROPHE FOR THE WEAK, STRUGGLING, LONELY, AND HURTING.

Alcorn has suggested that the minister must anticipate and prevent sexual temptations. Anonymity and leisure time spell catastrophe for the weak, struggling, lonely, and hurting.[10]

In two areas, traveling and counseling, a pastor must take precautions. If you are a pastor who travels, especially alone in ministry, take special care of the dangers inherent in such labor—being alone in a hotel room, spending long hours under no one's watchful observation, separated from your wife for days perhaps, and tempted in unusually aggressive ways. Practical attempts to "make no provision for the flesh" can and must be made. That may include blocking certain cable stations from the room TV set, bringing with you healthy reading material, or planning to complete church-related business in the room.

In developing relationships with counselees you must realize how easily emotional bonding can occur. In our efforts to empathize with those who hurt we pastors can enter into a warm and satisfying relationship that is very dangerous.

Jay Kesler, a counselor and college president, has warned, "The development of a warm relationship into one with sexual overtones can be very subtle, which makes it all the more dangerous; dealing with sexual temptation would be a lot easier if it were based just on physical desire, which is easier to recognize."[11]

What is the careful and wise shepherd to do? For starters you should make it a policy to avoid regular counseling situations with women in the church. Training and utilizing godly women in helping will free you from much potential danger. Further, decide in advance what you will do when you find yourself faced with a sexual situation, albeit one not so immediately obvious. One writer suggests that the pastor must use James 1:2–8, praying for true wisdom. As E. Stanley Jones said, "If you don't make up your mind, your unmade mind will unmake you."[12]

2. Understand the Power of the Seductive Woman

Under no circumstances is the pastor to be excused from the consequences of adulterous actions. When he sexually sins, as we saw earlier, he uses the very power of his office to abuse the parishioner he has become sexually involved with. There are times, however, when he must resist more overt temptation that comes to him through the power of seduction.

The woman who acts provocatively must be resisted without hesitation. The writer of Proverbs could be addressing pastors as well as the common man when he writes of the provocative woman:

> . . . to keep you from the evil woman, from the smooth tongue of the adulteress. Do not desire her beauty in your heart, nor let her catch you with her eyelids. Can a man take fire in his bosom, and his clothes not be burned? Or can a man walk on hot coals, and his feet not be scorched? So the one who goes in to his neighbor's wife; whoever touches her will not go unpunished. (6:24–25, 27–29)

This passage encourages the man to be careful of the flirtatious look of the woman who unduly seeks his attention. The pastor must be especially careful to guard himself when he detects the first mannerisms that indicate a woman may have feelings that are beyond those of a healthy and pure relationship.

Louis McBurney, founder of the Marble Retreat Center and a marriage counselor, stresses that a woman may use several approaches to lead a pastor into trouble; we pastors should recognize these. Included in his list are excessive praise, words expressing her loneliness and the need for sessions with the pastor only, and even attempts to initiate physical contact. He says, further, that signals within the pastor's life include his keeping her alive in his mind, making excuses to see her, and a willingness to share his own marital secrets with her.[13]

3. Guard Your Mind

The pastor needs to resist sexual fantasies aggressively if he would remain pure. Amazingly, the 1988 *Leadership* survey (see chapter 1) found that 39 percent of responding pastors regarded sexual fantasies as harmless. In the light of Matthew 5: 27–30, how can sexual fantasies be viewed as harmless? Such fantasies may be one of the principal doorways we open with our minds that can lead to overt sexual sin.

Professor and counselor David Seamands seems to understand the need to guard one's mind against the dangers of sexual temptations when he writes concerning Matthew 26:41, "I suspect he [Jesus] chose his words carefully because he knew that some temptations, including sexual attraction, are so powerful that after a certain point, the will gives in to the urge."[14]

The pastor must guard his mind by staying away from explicitly erotic material, as well as television programs and images that fuel the fires of lust. Meditating on Philippians 4:8 and Proverbs 4:14–15 will be of great help in this regard. Pornography surrounds us, acting as a poison that corrupts healthy sexuality. It had crippled and destroyed more than one otherwise effective pastoral ministry.

I urge pastors to consider an "eye covenant" (Job 31:1) to protect themselves from sexual impurity. Keep your eyes from wandering to images and even to dwelling on passing women that can entice with fantasies. As Alcorn notes, "A battering ram may hit a fortress a thousand times, and no one time seems to have an effect, yet finally the gate caves in." For most men, our thoughts are readily influenced by images, for we are visually oriented. When our thoughts are assailed visually time after time, we are more vulnerable, for "immorality is the cumulative product of small mental indulgences and minuscule compromises, the immediate consequences of which were, at the time, indiscernible," according to Alcorn. "Our thoughts are the fabric with which we weave our character and destiny."[15]

4. Cultivate and Protect Your Own Marriage

How important are our marriages as protection against sexual sin? "Without a doubt, being in love with our mates provides the best defense against a sexual affair," McBurney says.[16] And Alcorn calls each pastor to continually cultivate his own marriage and recollect fond memories of good times he has enjoyed with his family in order to prevent sexual sin.[17] Such care provides a wall of protection that keeps out illicit loves.

This seems to be the plainest meaning of the wisdom given in Proverbs 5:15–23: You must enjoy your wife physically and her alone. Ponder the words of those nine verses.

One pastor explained his ability to display sexual fidelity this way: "I decided early in my Christian life that I would not become sexually involved with any woman other than my wife. This has been tested a number of times and being satisfied with my wife has been a big motivating factor. She has met my needs for sex and intimacy." Another minister answered researchers by saying: "I believe the key [to avoiding an affair] is the relationship between husband and wife. It must take time and planning—a mutual respect and encouragement and good listening to each other's needs."[18]

In the past, society's disapproval as well as a trained Christian conscience were a general restraint upon marital infidelity. There was a time when leaders in almost any sphere were discredited if they violated their marriage bond openly. Not any more. Even pastors can now divorce their spouses and show up somewhere else in pastoral labor a year or two later. And this happens often with much support from the congregation. Many approve because they too are part of the tragic breakdown of marriage in our age. Others have been forced into silence because it is "unloving" to reject a man who has "been forgiven" of his adultery.

In previous decades even marriages that were far from "satisfying" were preserved because of loyalty to God and the covenant itself. Today this is less and less true. Unsatisfactory marriages are viewed as an opportunity for nurturing thoughts of something "better." Almost every extended family knows divorce, making it an easier option to consider.

"FIERCE LOYALTY" TO OUR WIVES IS A KEY TO GUARDING OUR MARRIAGE AGAINST FAILURE. SPEAK ONLY IN A POSITIVE AND EDIFYING WAY OF YOUR WIFE IN PUBLIC.

God desires that a pastor remain faithful to his wife, and if he is not satisfied with her then he must build into his relationship those qualities that will provide an atmosphere of hope. Even if change does not come, there are never grounds for fleeing to another woman.

"Fierce loyalty" to our wives is a key to guarding our marriage against failure. Speak only in a positive and edifying way of your wife in public. Be extremely careful in what you say to her and about her. Let her know that you esteem her highly in every way possible.

5. Take Precautions As You Minister

Be extremely careful where, when, and how you see women in your ministry routines. Be prepared for how you will respond in advance of any situation that might arise. Talk to other men who have insight to share, and remember the word "flee" when you are ever placed in a compromising situation.

The pastor needs to decide how and when he will meet with women for counseling. It is commonly agreed that counseling women in long-term relationships is detrimental for both the pastor and the woman involved. I have found it best over many years of pastoral ministry to never meet a woman alone in her home, and never in my office unless others are present. Generally, I ask for the husband's presence. More times than not I meet a woman in my own home with my wife present. I find that godly women both understand and respect this approach. Paul counsels us to "Make no provision for the flesh in regard to its lusts" (Roman 12:14b).

The pastor must be careful in dealing with young adults in general, especially singles and young married women. Discretion is needed for each situation. Extreme care is needed when any bodily contact is made with female members of the congregation. The "holy kiss" was abused early on in the history of the church, and in a sensual age like ours warnings need to be given again.

In working with other staff in the church the pastor must guard himself as well. You must be especially careful not to allow any situation to arise that will cause gossip, rumor, or innuendo, avoiding even the appearance of evil. Careful planning and discussion with staff will go a long way in protecting everyone in this regard. In the light of the high incidence of pastoral adultery with a member of the church staff I think this cannot be over emphasized.

If difficult situations arise in the normal routines of ministry, immediately inform your wife and probably one or two fellow leaders in the church. By keeping these individuals informed you protect yourself and get the safety of an "abundance of counselors [where] there is deliverance" (Proverbs 11:14). Simply put, the wise pastor cannot be overly careful.

6. Maintain Relationships
Where Accountability Is Real

Every pastor needs several relationships where he is mutually accountable for his actions and relationships with others. Develop a caring relationship where honesty prevails and openness is carefully cultivated and protected. The "faithful wounds of a friend" (Proverb 27:6), when administered properly in a loving relationship, are still useful for keeping us from serious failure.

In a survey taken among pastors one writes, "To survive, a minister needs accountability." Another pastor comments, "Those ministers I have known to have been unfaithful had no peer group to which they were accountable in a personal way."[19]

Most pastors who fall never set out to sin, certainly not in the way that they do. A pattern often emerges in which they become increasingly isolated and relationally independent. Structures of accountability are not clearly established by the pastor or the church. The results are often seen in a complete breakdown of ministry in a number of areas, one of which is sexual compromise.

7. Cultivate Your Spiritual, Emotional, and Physical Well-Being

The danger often begins with our ignoring our personal well-being. As pastors, we are so busy preparing, teaching, and preaching that we may neglect to care for our own souls. For some of us, we have no outlet for our emotions other than professional service and church-related ministry. Certainly a frenetic schedule does not help our physical well-being; our schedules may even subvert our health in a number of ways.

As a minister of the flock, you must know yourself and take care of your body and soul to remain strong. I can't help but believe that a man's prayer life, his reading of the Word of God, and his personal devotion declined severely long before he fell morally. He may have even kept up the practice of those personal disciplines, albeit in a rigid and disciplined manner, but his soul was starved of real friendship with God. He was satisfied with something other than joyful communion with the Savior in the power of the Holy Spirit.

8. Consider Regularly the Consequences of Sexual Sin

Develop, if not in writing, at least mentally, a list of the specific consequences of sexual adultery. What will this sin mean for your wife? Your children? Your congregation? Your closest friends? Your future ministry?

We need to do this because the outcome of this particular sin is so deceiving. "Like most other temptations infidelity promises rich enticements at very little cost. At the beginning of an affair hardly anyone will believe the tremendous pain that will be experienced in the coming months."[20]

When God gave Israel His commands in the Old Covenant era He often rehearsed the consequences of obedience and disobedience very plainly. Moses told certain tribes to stand on Mount Ebal and others on Mount Gerizim; then he told them that one group would represent the blessing for obedience and the other the curses for disobedience. God was graphically displaying the heavy penalty that sin extracted in peoples' lives, while He was also showing what blessings came as a result of obeying Him. Surely these were written for our benefit and instruction under the New Covenant, which offers a better pattern by virtue of the Holy Spirit's indwelling us (1 Corinthians 10:11).

THE CHURCH AND THE PASTOR TOGETHER

It is the church's responsibility to help in establishing a healthier environment for successful ministry. Further, the church needs to become more proactive in addressing the issues that can help to prevent pastoral moral failure.

Ultimately, however, the pastor alone is responsible for his choices and his personal life. Integrity can be maintained only by his earnest efforts to mortify his flesh. Your duty as pastor is to understand the times in which you serve and to avoid the pitfalls that can entrap you in sexual misconduct. You will go a long way toward preventing misconduct and moral failure by (1) keeping your own life strong before God in private, (2) nurturing your marriage, and (3) keeping continually before you the dangers associated with every decision you make.

NOTES

1. Hudson T. Armerding, "Christian Leadership," *Command,* Summer 1976, 8.

2. David Wang, "Church Leadership: Contrasts Between China and the West," *Evangelicals Now*, December 1991, 13.

3. Tim LaHaye, *If Ministers Fall, Can They Be Restored?* (Grand Rapids, Mich.: Zondervan, 1990), 51–52.

4. Jay Kesler, *Being Holy, Being Human* (Waco, Tex.: Word, 1988), 142–43.

5. Larry Chesser, "Prevention Best Protection in Sexual Misconduct Cases," *Illinois Baptist*, 5 January 1994, 7.

6. Ibid..

7. Bob Allen, "Pastoral Infidelity Takes Toll on Church," *Illinois Baptist,* January 1994, 7.

8. James Boyd Newton, "Pastor Immorality: Grounds for Permanent Disqualification" a D.Min. writing project, Temple Baptist Seminary, 1993, 109. I am indebted to this research for several of the thoughts contained in this section.

9. Randy Alcorn, "Strategies to Keep from Falling," *Leadership* 9 (Winter 1988): 49.

10. Randy Alcorn, *Sexual Temptation: How Christian Workers Can Win the Battle* (Downers Grove, Ill.: InterVarsity Press, 1989), 13–30.

11. Ibid., 144.

12. As quoted in Henry A. Virkler, *Broken Promises: Healing and Preventing Affairs in Christian Marriage* (Dallas: Word, 1992), 278.

13. Louis McBurney, "Avoiding the Scarlet Letter" *Leadership* 6 (Summer 1985): 48–50.

14. Archibald Hart, et al. "Private Sins of Public Ministry" *Leadership* 9 (Winter 1988): 15.

15. Randy Alcorn, "Strategies to Keep from Falling," 46.

16. Louis McBurney, "Avoiding the Scarlet Letter," 46.

17. Randy Alcorn, "Strategies to Keep from Falling," 44.

18. Jack Balswick and John Thoburn, "How Ministers Deal with Sexual Temptation" *Pastoral Psychology* 39: (May 1991) 281, 280.

19. Ibid., 283.

20. Henry A. Virkler, *Broken Promises*, 277.

CHAPTER TWELVE

SIX PROPOSALS AND A PLEA FOR REFORMATION

I believe that the imperative need of the day is not simply revival, but a radical reformation that will go to the root of our moral and spiritual maladies and deal with causes rather than with consequences, with the disease rather than with symptoms.

A. W. Tozer

*T*he Protestant Reformers believed that the visible church was to be found where three marks were present—a right preaching of the gospel, a right administration of the sacraments, and a right practice of church discipline. In our day the church needs desperately to recover this final mark of the holy church —proper discipline. I submit that all three marks are in disarray; yet the third is almost wholly lost to our generation. This book is prayerfully written as a serious and solemn call for the recovery of "the third mark of the church."[1]

Church reform and doctrinal recovery are needed in every generation. Our generation is no different. We have lost our way in large areas of biblical truth and practice. If we are to experience again the showers of divine mercy we must seek the reformation of the church while we pray for genuine awakening. The life of the church depends upon this. We are part of a living organism that does not thrive and grow unless it is conformable to the holy patterns of God's Word. These patterns have been proven by centuries of faithful practice. We must labor to recover these old paths.

Pastoral sexual misconduct plagues the modern church. We have not always heeded the Scriptures regarding discipline. I fear that Christ has something against us. As He spoke to the church in ancient Thyatira I wonder if He speaks in a similar fashion to many of our churches in the West:

> The Son of God, who has eyes like a flame of fire, and His feet are like burnished bronze, says this: "I know your deeds, and your love and faith and service and perseverance, and that your deeds of late are greater than at first. But I have this against you, that you tolerate the woman Jezebel, who calls herself a prophetess, and she teaches and leads My bond servants astray, so that they commit acts of immorality and eat things sacrificed to idols. And I gave her time to repent and she does not want to repent of her immorality." (Revelation 2:18–21)

What would our Lord say to the typical evangelical church in this age? To paraphrase the words of the apostle John in Revelation 2, He might say: "I have this against you. You tolerate sexual misconduct and the sexual abuse of members of My body. This is often carried out by pastors you have allowed to hurt my people. Indeed, you have grown to accept this as a normal problem and have carved out cisterns of your own for solving this problem. Your solutions lean heavily upon the wisdom of fallen men. If you will not repent I will give you over to even more immorality, and you will see the ultimate devastation that results from your conduct!"

THE IMPORTANCE OF PROPER DISCIPLINE

If the modern church is to recover again the marks of the visible church, she must restore the discipline of her pastors to the top of her agenda. How can we ever expect God to pour out blessing upon our flocks when we tolerate, and even tacitly approve, the sexual misconduct of our pastors?

Church discipline has always been at the forefront of any reformation period in the historic church. As we have previously noted, the great eras of church reformation and revival have always been concerned with the purity of the church. This purity begins in the leadership. The early church understood this well. The Protestant Reformers and Puritans restored this concern with even better biblical balance. The early American church leaders, as well as those impacted directly by the Great Awakening, saw this also. It is the very same principle seen in Nehemiah when he called upon Israel to forsake her false ways and return wholly to the Lord.

A growing chorus of evangelicals are calling for revival in our time. I rejoice in their concern; yet I am troubled. Such calls for revival often gloss over the appalling sins of our age, even as they become preoccupied with engaging the culture through political and social agendas. Sin is destroying our very witness before the world. Scandals internally will corrupt ministries. Our prayers for revival will not be heard until we "turn from our wicked ways" and "humble" ourselves (2 Chronicles 7:14).

My appeal is that we join our prayerful intercessions for revival with deliberate efforts for reformation—a reformation that seeks to bring the church back to moral purity in conformity with Scripture. All of our historic evangelical confessions of faith acknowledge this concern. Can we do less?

Dare we pray for revival and actually do less?

SIX PROPOSALS FOR REFORMATION

Your church and mine can be involved in such a reformation. As a modest summation of what we have seen in this book I would submit the following proposals for reformation in returning to moral purity. Each can be enacted by evangelical churches and associations.

1. Determine the Truth of the Charges

First, wherever suspicion exists that moral failure has taken place in the life of a pastor, wisdom and care must be taken by the leaders of a particular church to determine if the reports are true. The counsel of 1 Timothy 5:19–20 must be carefully followed as outlined in chapter 8. The specific charges must be heard in private first, with a body of several witnesses present to determine the nature and truthfulness of the charges. Those who entertain charges must give due consideration to the character and trustworthiness of those who have made the charges. Judgment should be withheld until all information has been received.

Then the evidence must be weighed. And should the charges not be substantiated, discipline for those who have leveled false accusations may very well become necessary.

The counsel of several other respected pastors from outside the church could very well be sought at a second stage of this process but preferably early in the unfolding of the process of investigation and response. Only when the facts are clearly ascertained can information be given publicly to the church, which in nearly every case must be done or the sin is not properly addressed in a biblical manner.[2]

2. Have Denominations and Associations Set Initiatives

Associations and denominations of churches need to establish, maintain, and support the kinds of initiatives that will allow and encourage proper investigation of all charges of moral failure. These can best be worked out in a manner agreeable to the polity of the respective church so that the process is both fair and firm.

3. Inform the Congregation When the Evidence Warrants

When charges of moral misconduct are proven to be true, the leaders must properly tell the congregation. The manner of how this is done will surely vary, (see page 172 for my proposal of public confession) but an agreeable approach should be established carefully. Great propriety is again called for as distinctions must be made between: (1) where a minister is wrongly accused and should be exonerated (even before the church if necessary to protect his reputation and ministry), (2) where the pastor admits the charge and displays a willingness to pursue a course of continual repentance, (3) where the pastor denies the charges but they are proven true beyond reasonable doubt, and (4) where, denying the charge, the pastor nevertheless is shown to have acted with serious impropriety or shown poor judgment. In this last case the pastor may still need to leave his office though his future will no doubt take a different direction than that of the man who has actually violated the seventh commandment.

Officers of the church should always act quickly but discreetly. They should never act in such a way as to draw undue attention to the sin itself. On the other hand, they should never give the flock the impression that sin in the leader can be countenanced. They must seek to establish and maintain an environment where members take such misconduct with utmost seriousness.

4. Remove the Guilty from Office

Pastors who are found guilty of sexual misconduct must immediately resign their office, or be removed if they fail to offer their resignation. They are disqualified from office because of their inability to be "above reproach." They have violated the sacred trust of their calling and thus should be stripped of ministerial standing in whatever way is appropriate.

To consider the question of setting a time period for return to office is a mistake for a number of reasons. As we noted previously, it jeopardizes the depth of the repentance needed. It also confuses the church's standard of purity in its leadership.

5. Help the Pastor Toward Restoration

Pastors removed from office should be helped, if repentant, to become responsible members of a local church once again. A process of restoration should be carefully undertaken, using several people (perhaps pastors from other congregations) to assist. The goal is to aid the former pastor in restoration to God, to the local church, and to proper relationship with his family; it is not restoration to his former office.

Such restoration probably will involve helping the former pastor develop a new career vocationally, assisting his family in adjusting to major changes, seeking to save the marriage where possible, and, in general, responding with compassion to each person directly affected by the pastor's moral failure. No time-table should be established, as each case is uniquely different.

The motivation for all of the above must be the glory of God. Those involved in the process must strive, with tears and patience, for the safeguarding of the principles of the Word of God.

6. Ask for Resignation If Leadership Is Damaged

In some cases, a moral indiscretion will not be established, but the pastor still should resign and depart the local church. If the pastor has lost his "good report" and is no longer viewed as "blameless" by his flock, he should consider resigning the church since he no longer has a basis for true spiritual minis-try in that particular flock. This may be the case in situations where the pastor has not been personally guilty of sexual sin, but sin within his own family or sin that has touched his lead-ership of the church directly weighs strongly against his hav-ing a future of effective ministry in the particular congre-gation. If he is a servant of the church and the church cannot properly accept his leadership without serious doubt and suspi-cion, I submit that his leadership is over whether he realizes it or not.

In some cases a "leave of absence" might help resolve some of these kinds of tensions, but the pastor should always realize that he is the servant of the church, not the chief execu-tive officer of a corporation. His name should always be cleared, if he is not guilty, but effective ministry might well end at the same time.

Ministry is totally a matter of character. It demands trust and confidence in the ability of the shepherd to guide and nur-ture through teaching the Word of God. The flock must be able to see that what the pastor teaches is true in his own life. When this no longer exists he should be advised to see the hand of providence guiding him elsewhere. Whether he is to blame or not, when his marriage breaks down, or his family is in complete disarray, he will find it hard to lead by clear and obvious example, especially when others have seen these developments come about in the church he is presently pastoring.

THE NEED FOR CONSISTENCY

The lack of uniformity regarding handling these kinds of situations is of major concern. Men can leave a church, move some distance away (sometimes only across the same town) and begin again as if nothing ever happened. This may mean the new church has handled the former pastor's discipline differently (or ignored it) than the former one. It may mean his previous church was not wholly open and complete in supplying a character reference regarding the former minister.

Churches in our time seem to have lost a sense of the seriousness of all sin. They are often unaware of the damage that is done by sexually adulterous pastors. Church boards are almost entirely unaware of the legal ramifications that presently surround this problem.

Further, church members often let their hearts and emotions overrule the Word of God. We have not taught people how to think through the teaching of 1 Timothy 3 and Titus 1. I can still remember hearing the member of a nominating committee saying, "Well, the next thing you know, this pastor will insist that we seriously apply the requirements of 1 Timothy 3," as if we could unseriously apply them.

Part of the church's proper response will be found in the pastor himself. Sheep follow the shepherding they receive. If what they have received for decades is shallow they often do not know the difference. Those who pastor them must begin to teach plainly and carefully regarding church discipline and the high ethical standards required of those who would lead the flock.

This is costly and painful work. A. W. Tozer spoke prophetically when he said, "Could it be that too many of God's true children, and especially the preachers, are sinning against God by guilty silence? . . . I for one am waiting to hear the loud voices of the prophets and reformers sounding once more over a sluggish and drowsy church. They'll pay a price for their boldness, but the results will be worth it."[3]

Churches sometimes fear giving attention to problems that will create complications beyond their experience. As a result they tend to take the "out of sight, out of mind" approach to difficult moral and ethical issues. This must be resisted lovingly and firmly.

What About Restoration to Office?

Should the sexually fallen pastor be returned to office at some future point?

I have argued that under almost every circumstance the answer should be no. I have labored to display reasons throughout this book. I will conclude with a simple summary:

1. The nature of the call to the pastoral ministry demands that the pastor remain faithful to his call or give it up if he discredits it.

2. The minister is a public figure and thus must maintain a consistent public example.

3. The world tends to judge the gospel by the lives of those who preach it and the church by its leadership.

4. Because many fallen leaders fall again if they remain in office, or return to office later, it is best to maintain the purity of the office and protect the church by not allowing such men to take leadership of the flock. Ask yourself and answer honestly: Can such a man be fully trusted in everything in the future, having violated his promise to be trustworthy when he was ordained?

5. The emphasis of the Scripture on moral purity is so strong and clear that being "above reproach" is not simply an initial requirement but obviously an ongoing one for those who hold pastoral office.

6. This sin is one of serious treachery. It displays an almost total lack of moral and spiritual judgment. How can a man who has sinned in such a manner meaning-

fully regain that which he has so willfully flung away in a season of almost unparalleled foolishness?

7. This sin, as proven earlier, is in a category of grave seriousness. It eats at a man's entire being in such a way that his character is irreparably harmed. He will always be known as an adulterer, no matter how he lives in the years to come. To insist that forgiveness is all that matters is to ignore the biblical emphasis upon proven godliness required of those who would shepherd the flock of Christ.

8. This sin is a direct attack upon the very image of Christ's love for the church (Ephesians 5). As Christ is the bridegroom of the church, and loves and protects her, so the husband is to love and cherish his wife. If we allow men to lead the church who recklessly throw away the divine pattern in their own lives how can we expect the bride to remain holy and profoundly in love with the Bridegroom Himself?

Ours is not the first generation to experience the deep wounds of moral failure within the church and its pastoral leadership. Our hope in the face of this present crisis of misconduct is not to be found, ultimately, in ourselves. We must cry out to God on behalf of Christ's church and plead with God to heal us as taught in Revelation 2:3. When Israel suffered through a time of moral and spiritual declension, God counseled her to repent and to return to a gracious God. That was a *corporate* event.

The words of Joel 2:14 are appropriate. "Who knows," says the prophet, God might even give us blessing in a great revival of godliness and fresh power from on high.

I urge all who love the cause of Zion to pray for the church—"who knows," God may come once again with healing and great blessing even as we address the awful pain of sexually fallen pastors biblically and more directly.

NOTES:

1. The loss of this third mark of the church and its importance to holiness is described in Art Azurdia, "Recovering the Third Mark of the Church" *Reformation & Revival Journal*, 3: 4 (Fall 1994). The article introduces the reader to the need for discipline and how to go about it. Azurdia argues cogently and biblically. A copy of the journal is available from: Reformation & Revival Ministries, Inc., P.O. Box 88216, Carol Stream, Illinois, 60188.

2. Ibid. Azurdia argues that the steps to be noted in Scripture are: (1) A confidential meeting; (2) A confidential meeting with witnesses; (3) A public explanation and exhortation to the church family; (4) A severing of fellowship. Discipline, especially of errant pastors, "deepens the church's commitment to self-purification" and "reinforces the true nature of body life."

3. A. W. Tozer, *God Tells the Man Who Cares*, (Camp Hill, Pa.: Christian Publications, 1970), 145.